Book Description

Are you finding it difficult to feel engaged and motivated after a breakup. Are you struggling with self-doubt, uncertainty, frustration, and other intense emotions that feel like they're out of control? Are you desperate to get back together with your ex no matter how many friends and family members discourage the idea, or are you feeling tempted to swear off love forever?

If so, this is exactly the book you need to teach you how to get over lost love, let go of your grief, and start moving forward with your life.

The death of a relationship can be just as devastating as the death of a loved one, as in essence you are learning to live without someone who was previously so important to you. It is difficult to get over a broken heart, and it can be even more difficult if you had a complicated or toxic relationship prior to your breakup. Getting over a crush can be equally tricky. In any of these cases, you may struggle with common issues like an inability to reign in your emotions and frequent self-critical thoughts. These issues can undermine your ability to move on after a breakup and prevent you from recognising all the experiences and accomplishments waiting for you throughout the rest of your life.

Of course, one bad breakup doesn't mean you're unlovable, nor does it mean your life needs to come to a screeching halt. In fact, a breakup can become an opportunity for you to grow and rediscover your passions in life once you have given yourself the time to heal and process your grief. When you start looking forward rather than looking back, you'll see just how bright of a future you have lying ahead of you.

In *How Do You Get Over Someone?* you'll find information and advice to help you move past a breakup and start the next chapter of your life, including:

- How to better understand and accept your feelings after a breakup
- How to get over someone you loved
- What to expect from the relationship grieving process and how to manage these intense emotions
- How to use the focus, control, and purpose (FCP) tripod method to feel more balanced in your life
- Examples of how to navigate the fallout from a toxic relationship and rediscover yourself

It's never easy to accept the end of a relationship, but this is a necessary step in order to move on. The sooner you begin the process of getting over someone you love after a breakup, the sooner you can begin a journey of self-discovery, recovery, and self-improvement. This will help you not only get over your old relationship, but also learn to recognise the value you have as an individual as you pursue your own success and happiness.

Don't let your breakup consume another day of your life. It's time to get over your ex, focus on yourself, and take control of your life once more.

THIS BOOK BELONGS TO:

_____

_____

Thank you for purchasing this book. If you enjoyed this title, then feedback on Amazon would be greatly appreciated. If you are not satisfied with this book, then drop us an e-mail at **priscilla@samaritanguidance.com**, and we will do our best to sort the problem.

MY DEAR READER, I LOVE YOU SO MUCH!

How do you get Over Someone?

A-to-Z on how to get Over Lost Love, how to get Over Someone you Loved, Getting Over Someone you Love, Getting Over a Crush, get Over a Broken Heart

(The Get Over Relationship Book Series)

Priscilla Nicchi

Table of Contents

Introduction

In the world of romance, the possibility of heartbreak is an unfortunate but often unavoidable problem. Very few people end up marrying the first person they date, and even fewer manage to make a single relationship last for the rest of their lives. Being in a relationship can allow you to experience incredible highs, but if you end up breaking up with someone you thought you would love forever, it will be all the more difficult to bear the pain of separation. This situation is further complicated if the relationship you shared was complicated or even toxic, which can make moving on even more complicated than usual. What is there to do now? Should you prepare yourself for the possibility of mourning your lost relationship forever? Is it time to swear off love for good?

While all relationships have their ups and downs and some end in a breakup, this doesn't mean that you'll never be able to love again, nor does it mean you'll feel as low as you do now for the rest of your life. It might feel like it, but the end of a relationship is not the end of the world, and it's important to avoid putting your life on hold or doing anything drastic like letting go of the possibility of finding love again. This is a difficult time in your life, but if you focus on healing and spend some time reflecting on who you are and who you want to be as an individual, not just as part of a matching set, you can come out of the experience with a renewed sense of self-love, a more positive outlook, and a better understanding of yourself.

It may not seem like it right now, but the end of a relationship can actually provide the perfect opportunity to do some self-discovery while you focus on coming to terms with what happened, and eventually moving on from your heartbreak. Oftentimes you will find that you learn the most about yourself in your darkest moments. All the distress and the emotionally charged nature of the situation provides you with an opportunity to grow inside and develop as a person so that you can become the best possible version of yourself. As you continue to grow, the pain of losing the relationship will fade, and you'll be able to take the next steps of your life with a renewed sense of freedom, following your personal path wherever it takes you.

In *How do you get Over Someone?*, you'll learn how to handle the pain and grief that comes with the end of a relationship without becoming self-destructive. You will start by getting a better sense of your feelings, however complicated they may be, and processing the complex web of emotions that going through a breakup can cause. Then, you'll learn about the "FCP tripod method," where FCP stands for Focus-Control-Purpose. You can use this method to ease the hurt you feel and start moving on, all while building up your self-confidence and continually improving yourself. A bad breakup is something you must give yourself time and space to fully mourn and come to terms with, but it's also a chance to embrace the necessity of change as a natural part of life. This is something I learned through first-hand experience, and it's a lesson I want to share with you so you can start to finally let go of your grief.

I previously experienced a bad breakup of my own, so I know exactly how it feels to end a relationship you believed would last forever. Even though I loved my ex-husband, our relationship had become toxic, and I was emotionally dependent on him for reassurance and validation. I was finding it difficult to maintain my sense of self, but even after my divorce, it still seemed equally if not more difficult to learn how to become my own person. I needed to regain control over my life, and I used change as a tool to overcome the hardships I was experiencing. Additionally, I found that the more I studied and taught psychology to help heal others' wounds after their bad breakups, the better I felt about my own breakup, and the easier it was for me to come to terms with my new reality.

My goal in writing this book is to enable you to find the peace of mind I finally achieved without all of the trial and error. Any breakup is the end of an era in your life, but it doesn't have to be the end of your life. You can learn and grow from the experience; you will come out the other side a completely new person who is more capable, independent, and hopeful. You only need to learn how to take your grief and process it into a positive driving force in your life.

Chapter 1: A Story

In order to understand my perspective on the end of relationships and why I believe I can help you get over your bad breakup, I want to begin by telling you a story about my own experiences. Through this, I want to help you see that even when things seem their most dire, you can still find relief from your woes and come out the other side a stronger, more confident, and more capable person.

I first met my ex-husband, Roberto, when I was in college at Bologna. At the time, I was immediately taken in by him. I knew we were perfect together, and I wanted nothing more than to be in a relationship with him for the rest of my life. Roberto was romantic and very engaged in our relationship, and it was clear that he would be the one for me. I was in college to pursue a literature major, but as our relationship got more serious, my plans for my future started to fizzle out, replaced with a desire to support Roberto's success instead. I ended up dropping out of my major program to get more serious about our relationship. We quickly got married and I became a housewife as Roberto expected of me, and he continued to study and eventually graduate. I believed Roberto would support both of us, so during this time, I saw nothing wrong with putting my previous goals on the backburner in favour of his success.

Despite our initial starry-eyed, passionate romance, things became less ideal after the marriage. Roberto had a passive-aggressive personality, and he would frequently make thinly veiled comments about my habits. He started to show a lack of self-confidence, which he often took out on me in the form of frequent arguments and criticisms. He would occasionally get aggressive during these conversations, and he would pick fights over how I dressed and spoke with friends. I started to feel like he was trying to control me, rather than feeling like an equal partner in our relationship. While there were still many moments of passionate reconciliation between the two of us, these seemed like small high points in between deep valleys of vicious arguments, and we could never find that same sense of balance and understanding we had at the very beginning of the relationship.

Unfortunately, things only got worse from there. After about two years of marriage, Roberto's need to be in control continued to increase to the point where I felt there was little I could do that didn't step out of line in some way. He grew more possessive and envious, and I started rarely spending time with friends out of a desire to avoid angering him. We had previously been a happy, loving couple who frequently travelled the world together and who had a large group of close friends, but every day we became more and more isolated. We no longer went on trips together, we avoided making plans with friends, and even the atmosphere inside the home had changed significantly. Neither of us was happy, but I found it especially difficult to deal with the relationship during this time as Roberto had deemed some of my friends 'dangerous' and prohibited me from being around them. Even though I loved him, his behaviour had become too controlling, and I knew that we were on the brink of a serious falling out.

I knew I had to leave the relationship for my own health, safety, and sanity. About two and a half years after getting married, shortly after Roberto's behaviour got worse, I left the house. I spent some time on my own, but I was so used to having Roberto around to direct what I should and shouldn't do that I found it hard to regain control over my life. Additionally, I had never completed my studies, so it was difficult to find employment that paid enough to support myself. When Roberto came to me and asked me to return, contrite and loving just like he was during one of the many 'honeymoon' periods that were interspersed with more aggressive conflicts, I relented and agreed to resume our matrimony. I hoped that things would be different and that this was just a small bump in the road, and we could bridge the gap between us.

I hoped that having children might help to "save our relationship," as I had heard before. I believed that perhaps if Roberto had the chance to be a loving father, he would come to adore me again, just like he had at the beginning of our relationship. However, I was unsuccessful at getting pregnant after months of trying, and this put an even greater strain on the relationship than before. Roberto blamed me for our inability to have children, and he felt resentment that I couldn't provide him with the family he desired. All the troubles we were having left me conflicted about Roberto and my place in my own life. I loved him, but I hated him at the same time. I cared for him, but I could hardly stand to be around him, and I bristled at his attempts to control me.

Our disagreements only worsened as we ran into some financial trouble. While money issues can divide even the healthiest of couples, we were far from healthy, to begin with, and having to stress about who was spending too much money and what we were going to do about our bills was only amplifying our usual arguments. During this time, I managed to convince Roberto to pick up some part-time work as a private language tutor for high school teenagers. This seemed like a benign decision at the time, but it eventually led to my realisation that things could change and that this relationship, as much as I wanted it to succeed, just wasn't working.

I ended up becoming close friends with one of the student's mothers, Emilia. Emilia understood my situation almost immediately, and she knew something was wrong and that things could not stay this way forever. She was a guide and a mentor to me when I needed it most, helping me understand the gravity of what I was experiencing and why it needed to end. She enabled me to find the courage to end the relationship, despite how difficult it was for me to let go of someone who had hurt me but who I still loved, and she helped me pick up the pieces of my life when I finally managed to divorce

Roberto. It was incredibly hard for me to get over him, both because of the love I still held for him and the control he exerted over my life for so long. I often found it difficult to motivate myself and to find ways to support myself now that I was on my own, but I knew that with her support, I was never really alone after all. With her counselling, I was able to come to terms with the extent of the abuse I had experienced during my relationship and to acknowledge my feelings, move past them, and embrace the life that was waiting for me on the other side.

Emilia's support inspired me to fulfil the same role for others. I became focused on living for myself, not for the approval of a partner. While I remained open to the possibility of a future relationship, I avoided throwing myself into one just for the sake of not being alone, and I instead took time to pursue my passions. For me, this meant finding my purpose in helping other people, at first as a private tutor and later as a therapist. I wanted to make sure other people in difficult situations knew they could experience a higher quality of life; these dark times did not have to be permanent if they had the strength and courage to make changes in their lives. I was especially interested in helping people through complicated relationships and bad breakups, since this was such a core part of my own experiences. As I continued to improve my knowledge and sense of self-respect, I helped others to do the same, since I know how devastating leaving a relationship can be but also how rewarding it is to find true happiness in life. Eventually, I graduated as a therapist, welcomed love back into my life with a new husband, and moved to London, where I work with women and families.

While the initial breakup with my husband was devastating due to my mixed feelings, I was able to make it through because I followed a process that helped me acknowledge my guilt while also encouraging me to move forwards with my life. It is this method that helped me pick up the pieces of my life and put them back together, and this is the method I will teach to you throughout this book so you can get over your past relationship. You may have doubts and fears; these are normal, and I had them too. But you cannot allow these worries to hold you back from truly experiencing your life. When you start coming to terms with how you feel about the end of your relationship, you can finally start to move on in a healthy, constructive way.

Chapter 2: Understanding Your Feelings

The end of a relationship can bring on many negative emotions, and you may not be entirely certain how to manage them. You'll likely feel lost, hurt, confused, upset, angry, and even ashamed at different times, and these emotions can be even more distressing when they're intermingled with feelings of relief and happiness that a relationship that no longer brought you joy is now over. While it can seem contradictory to feel this way, it's actually perfectly normal, and it does much more harm than good to ignore your emotions no matter what you may be feeling.

Your emotions are a part of you, whether you accept them or not. They can affect the way you perceive certain situations, leading you to feel joyful or depressed, and if you don't confront them, they will simply simmer under the surface until you can't control them anymore. This leads to outbursts and erratic behaviour, and you may end up accidentally hurting someone you love or committing acts of self-sabotage. Worse, if you don't understand what you're feeling, this can lead you to take the wrong actions to resolve these emotions. You might engage in harmful and self-destructive coping mechanisms, all because you are still wrestling with your feelings about a prior negative experience and you're not sure where to begin dealing with them.

The first step in learning to bring these emotions under control and to express them in a safe and healthy way is understanding what they are and why you may be experiencing them. Some common feelings you may experience after the difficult end of a relationship are a loss of identity, low self-esteem, feelings of failure, anxiety and depression, loss of security, and other negative responses. Before you can understand how to manage these reactions, you must first learn about why they're occurring and how they play into the greater grieving process.

Loss of Identity

When you're in a relationship, you may begin to mould your identity around the idea of being partners with someone else. You start to define yourself as someone's spouse, or their boyfriend or girlfriend. When you picture the future of your life, you likely picture them in it. You also get comfortable with the idea of being someone's romantic partner and making this trait a core part of yourself. All this means that once that relationship ends, it's very common to struggle to define yourself as an individual, not just as someone who is in a relationship.

Most couples spend time together very frequently. You might have seen each other three or more days in an average week, and you likely texted or called each other almost every day, at least for the majority of your relationship before the breakup. If you were married, you woke up next to someone else, you came home to them after work, and you fell asleep next to them, meaning they were your biggest constant throughout the day. If you no longer have this person in your life, you may struggle to understand what you want to do now that they're not around. What kind of food do you like when you're not subconsciously thinking about what someone else wants to eat? What sort of movies do you enjoy watching alone rather than with your partner? What is your career going to look like, and where do your true passions lie? Are there parts of yourself that you have been suppressing in order to better fit into a relationship, and if so, how do you go about embracing these aspects of your true personality now that you have the freedom to do so?

These questions become even more relevant if you experienced an especially messy breakup, or abuse of any kind. If your partner attempted to control who you spent your time with and where you were allowed to go, it can be uncomfortable trying to engage in these forbidden activities again. During the relationship, you became dependent on someone else to tell you how to behave, and it's often very challenging to decide how you want to move forwards when you have a newfound sense of agency over your life. You may have even attempted to change parts of your personality to better suit your partner, but now that they're not in your life anymore, you'll need to rediscover these missing parts of yourself. This can be a difficult journey full of turmoil because it feels like you don't quite know who you are anymore, but it is a journey worth taking if you want to quell these feelings of having lost a piece of your identity.

Low Self-Esteem

After a breakup, you may find yourself wondering where you went wrong and what you could have done to regain their love. You might ask yourself questions like, "What did I do to make him hate me?" or "Why doesn't she love me anymore?" If you choose to place the blame for the breakup on yourself, each of these kinds of questions is going to harm your self-esteem, as you're framing the breakup in a way that suggests you could have maintained the relationship if only you were better or more lovable. This ignores the fact that sometimes people simply drift apart, or there are other circumstances that interfere with a relationship remaining healthy and consensual. Of course, when you are completely overtaken by your emotions, rational thought tends to take a back seat. These doubts about your self-worth take hold even though you may logically know that they're unfair and untrue. You need someone to blame for the end of the relationship, so you decide to lay the blame at your own feet, regardless of how unhealthy this kind of thinking may be.

Unfortunately, having a low sense of self-esteem can negatively impact many parts of your life. For one, you may find it difficult to consider that someday you may decide to start a relationship with someone new again. You could begin to see yourself as unworthy of being loved and unlikeable by any possible romantic partners. You might also find that your productivity suffers at work or school, as you start constantly doubting yourself and being critical of everything you do. You're more likely to feel stressed out when something doesn't go your way and to blame your own incompetence whenever anything goes wrong. You might decide to let good opportunities pass you by because you don't feel like you're capable enough to handle them, and you're worried you're just going to mess everything up. Every mistake and negative interaction becomes another reinforcement of your critical beliefs about yourself, to the point that you might struggle to find anything good about yourself, ignoring all of the positive qualities you possess. It is often difficult to leave this mindset behind as you begin the healing process, but as you start coming to terms with the ending of your relationship, you'll find it easier to forgive yourself and highlight all the parts of yourself that you love instead.

Feelings of Having Failed

If you were very committed to staying with someone for the rest of your life, the end of your relationship with them can feel like you have failed. Relationships require a lot of effort from both parties. There are times when you might make compromises and do things you wouldn't otherwise consider, all because you are so committed to making sure the relationship succeeds. You may have had moments near the end of the relationship where you knew you would do anything if it meant your partner would stay, and yet the relationship ended anyway. This can lead you to place all the blame for the outcome on yourself, even though your partner is equally culpable in determining the course of any relationship.

Additionally, defining a relationship in terms of 'success' and 'failure' can be self-defeating. If you consider any relationship that doesn't end to be successful, does this mean that achieving this idea of success is more important than prioritising your health and wellbeing? This line of thinking could lead you to stay in an abusive or otherwise imbalanced relationship for a long time just because you want to avoid failure. This is, of course, a misunderstanding of what you should be pursuing when you enter a relationship. You want to achieve a healthy partnership where you both enjoy each others' company and you're happy to be together. If you aren't happy in a relationship, whether this is due to a power imbalance or just a difference in personality and life goals, this isn't exactly a success story. There's no need to make yourself miserable just for the sake of prolonging a relationship. Even if you are happy during your relationship, breaking up doesn't have to mean that you failed. Instead, it is more of an opportunity to reflect on yourself and grow as a person, which is far from what most people would consider failure. In order to heal and move forward, you'll need to let go of these feelings of failure and stop beating up on yourself.

Anxiety and Depression

Relationships can often be a source of stress, and no period of time is more stressful than during and shortly after a breakup. All this stress can culminate in mental health issues and contribute to an increased likelihood of developing anxiety, depression, or symptoms of both conditions. Both anxiety and depression can affect the way you approach certain issues, how you think of yourself, and what kind of behaviours you engage in after your relationship ends.

Anxious thoughts are often symptomatic of doubts and fears you hold about yourself. You may no longer feel capable in your abilities, and you may feel uncertain performing certain activities that you used to do with your partner. Something as simple as going to the grocery store can become a reminder that you now have to do this task alone, and therefore a reason to feel anxious as you attempt to complete it. A bad breakup can severely worsen already existing social anxiety, as you experience a loss of confidence about your ability to create and maintain social relationships. You might tell yourself that if you couldn't manage to keep your romantic partner interested enough to stick around, then there's little chance anyone else wants to spend time with you either, which can cause you to further isolate yourself during an already isolating time in your life. While a little bit of anxiety in the weeks following a breakup is fairly common, anxiety that doesn't improve or gets worse as time goes on is a cause for concern, as it can quickly develop into a serious roadblock in your personal growth and development.

Depressive thoughts are equally common after a bad breakup, but like anxiety, they can become something to worry about if left untreated. Mild depression can dampen your enthusiasm for activities you previously enjoyed, especially if they're things you used to do with your ex. It can feel difficult to motivate yourself to complete your tasks because your thoughts are often preoccupied. In some cases, this moderate form of depression can increase the number of critical thoughts you direct towards yourself, making your mental state even worse. More severe forms of depression may include persistent negative self-talk that contributes to a low self-image, an inability to manage your everyday tasks that previously weren't an issue, and in some cases, even moments of suicidal ideation. If you feel that your depression has grown out of control and you're worried you might harm yourself, speak to a mental health professional as soon as possible, or contact an emergency hotline for assistance.

It is difficult to overcome anxiety and depression, whether they come from a breakup or another source of stress and uncertainty in your life, but it's never impossible. These kinds of negative thoughts often arise because life has lost some of its lustres, and you're a little uncertain about where to go from here. As you start making self-improvements and looking for new ways to feel more engaged in the world around you, you'll start to let go of some of these ideas and feelings that would otherwise hold you back from truly enjoying your future. You can learn to put anxiety and depression to bed while coming to terms with your newly-single status.

Loss of Security

Many people describe their partner as their rock. They look to them to help make difficult decisions, and they're relying on them in times of turmoil. Because of this, when a breakup occurs, you may feel like you've lost your foundation. Having strong social connections is very important for everyone. We are social creatures by our very nature, and relationships are just as necessary to our survival as other basics like food and shelter. Therefore, it feels very foreign when we suddenly lose one of the connections that we depended upon so heavily. It's common to feel insecure after a breakup, both in regards to yourself and how you fit into the wider world around you, because a strong bond has just been broken.

Oftentimes, "the grief [you] experience after a breakup has a lot in common with the grief that follows the death of a loved one" (Cleveland Clinic, 2019, para. 1). It's possible you may not see this person again for a long while, if you ever see them again at all. Someone you once spent a great deal of time with is now almost entirely gone from your life in most cases, which can make it incredibly difficult to continue feeling secure in the status of your other relationships. You may worry about your friends and family leaving you behind as well, fearing the thought of losing them just like you lost your partner.

In some cases, you might still see your ex fairly frequently. For example, if you work with them or go to school together, it may be impossible for you to avoid each others' company. Rather than helping you heal, this repeated exposure can actually deepen the wound left by the breakup. If you can grieve for a lost relationship just like you can grieve for a lost loved one, then seeing your ex around frequently feels like seeing their ghost. They're still present, but the dynamic of your relationship has changed on a fundamental level, and it can be incredibly difficult to move on with your life when you have to face reminders of your previous relationship every day. All of this contributes to a loss of security and greater feelings of distress and uncertainty.

In short, your relationship was once your security blanket, and now this security blanket has been torn away from you. It's understandable to feel a little lost at this point in your life, as you're not certain what you should do next, or how to go about your life now that you're no longer part of a conjoined pair. This is a very isolating feeling, but like the others we have discussed so far, it doesn't have to continue holding you back if you choose to heal instead.

Other Roadblocks to Recovery

The issues discussed so far are fairly common experiences after a breakup, but they're far from the only ways a breakup can affect your life. Additional effects tend to mirror those you might expect to see from people who are grieving a loved one. For example, you might find it harder to motivate yourself or to stay focused on a given task, whether it's something you're doing for enjoyment or for work or school. Even though you know that staying productive is important, especially if your job or grades depend on it, distracting and depressing thoughts can often break your concentration, making it more difficult to get anything done.

In some cases, you may feel angry after a relationship ends. You might direct this anger at your ex, yourself, the world at large, or any bystanders who happen to catch you in a bad mood. This can then lead to guilt when you have a clearer head and you start to regret snapping at people who were only trying to help you. Anger can often cause you to commit self-destructive acts out of a feeling of desperation, so it's important to bring this anger under control before it can do any damage to your remaining relationships.

Sometimes the end of a relationship can also carry a sense of relief. In the vast majority of cases, relationships don't simply end out of the blue, even if it may feel this way some days. Instead, small fractures and moments of tension make themselves known for weeks or months before the eventual breakup. When you get out of a particularly messy relationship, you may feel relieved that you no longer have to worry about resolving your relationship issues anymore. This can be distressing because it seems to run counter to the idea that you truly loved your ex, even though this isn't necessarily true. You can love someone and still recognise that a relationship isn't working or isn't healthy, and it's time to move on for the sake of your wellbeing. While you may experience some guilt, there's really no reason to be ashamed. Like everything we have mentioned so far, these feelings will eventually fade with time and a commitment to healing.

Tackling Emotional Problems

Understanding what you're currently feeling is just one piece of the puzzle. The next step is to put this improved understanding to work, using it to target the sources of your distress and start to ease some of your suffering. Remind yourself that these feelings are not permanent, and you will move past them in time. As you follow the advice laid out in future chapters, you'll start to see how you can progress through the different phases of your grieving period, come to terms with what's happened, and eventually achieve a sense of inner peace, leaving these confusing and self-defeating emotions behind.

Chapter 3: Mechanisms of Grief

The end of a relationship is a significant loss in your life, and it carries with it the same weight as many other kinds of substantial losses. A common misconception about grief is that the only people who experience it are those who are reeling from the death of a loved one, but this just isn't true. In fact, grief can arise in many different situations that involve loss. These include the loss of your health, the end of a friendship, losing your job, no longer being financially secure, retiring, moving, and of course, after a breakup. While the severity and exact experiences of your grief can differ depending on the situation, it's not unusual to go through the grieving process after a breakup. By understanding the loss of your relationship through the lens of grief, you can translate your intense, often confusing emotions into something more understandable and familiar; you will then have a better position from which to handle these feelings.

Grief in the way we understand it today is centred around five stages or phases of mourning. This idea was pioneered and popularised by Elisabeth Kübler-Ross, a psychiatrist who worked closely with terminally ill patients. She found that while everyone experiences and handles grief a little differently, there are five general stages that most people progress through as they attempt to come to terms with the newfound sense of loss in their lives. In her 1969 book *On Death and Dying*, Kübler-Ross wrote about the mental stages these terminally ill patients experienced, these being denial, anger, bargaining, depression and finally, acceptance (Kübler-Ross, 1969). While this order was commonly observed in her research, the progression of grief is often not nearly so linear. You might experience the stages in a different order, repeat some stages, or skip over some stages entirely. Still, the Kübler-Ross model can be an effective stepping stone for better understanding yourself during your darkest moments. You'll know what to expect in your near future if you're in the earlier stages of grief, and you'll develop an improved idea of how to handle any difficult emotions you might currently be experiencing so you can achieve acceptance.

Denial

Denial in the standard grief model refers to the idea of rejecting a diagnosis of a terminal illness. In a more general sense, it means refusing to acknowledge death or another form of loss as true. For a period of time after your relationship ends, you may struggle to believe that it's really over. You may convince yourself that you only have to say or do the right thing, and your partner will come rushing back into your arms again. You may believe that they'll realise they've made a mistake and take everything back, and the two of you can go back to how things were before. You might even continue acting as though you're still in a relationship, at times even forgetting that the relationship ended until reality comes crashing back in.

Denial is typically one of the earliest if not the first stage of grief because it involves refusing to acknowledge that there's anything to grieve at all. It typically precedes phases like bargaining and depression because there's little to bargain with or become depressed about if you can't fully conceive of the idea that the breakup occurred. Therefore, overcoming this stage merely means accepting the fact that you are no longer in a relationship. However, this is often not as easy as it sounds, as you might have already found out for yourself.

Oftentimes, our brains can trick us into maintaining this denial period as a sort of self-defence mechanism so we don't have to confront the harsh reality of the situation. We jump to denial because if we accepted that a relationship was over with no hope of recovery right away, we would feel completely adrift, unable to accept what has happened to us and having no idea of where we should go from here. It is overwhelming to receive and process all this information at once, so we allow ourselves a brief period of reprieve, typically by shutting out the truth and refusing to acknowledge or accept it. While this might be a more comfortable way to live, and it's certainly easier for us to handle, this completely prevents us from coming to terms with what occurred and finding the strength to move forward. We cannot process something that we are still in denial about, so it is necessary to let this denial go before you can do any serious healing.

Accepting Reality

Facing facts is often difficult to do. There's a good chance you'd prefer to believe that maybe someday soon you will get back together with your ex, or that the whole breakup was just a big misunderstanding and there's still a chance. Accepting reality is difficult, but of course, necessary. Still, if you're having trouble acknowledging the truth of the situation, there are a few methods you can use to let go of your doubts and tear the wool from your eyes.

The first step is to allow yourself to feel any emotions you have about the situation honestly. It's okay to feel hurt, angry, and upset. These feelings are completely natural, as are the other feelings covered in the previous chapter. Denying your emotions can have just as damaging of an effect as denying the truth, and you do yourself no favours by pretending like these feelings don't exist. You only make it more difficult to process them and deal with them in a healthy way. As you start to let these emotions in, you'll likely move on to other phases of grief, but it is only through understanding how you feel that you can start to work towards accepting it.

Another important step is to stop checking up on what your ex is doing or how they seem to be getting on without you. You may feel tempted to stalk them on social media, checking to see if they've already moved on and found someone else, or if they're feeling just as bad as you are. This tendency only feeds into your denial about your relationship being over, making it an unhealthy behaviour. The more you allow your ex to become a part of your daily routine, even through the barrier of social media, the harder it is for you to really move on. If you find you can't control yourself, try unfriending them, logging out of your social media profiles, or asking a trusted friend to change your passwords so you don't have access to your account for a few days. Even this brief separation can make it easier to withstand the temptation to check up on them in the future.

Separation in the digital world is just one step for ridding your life of reminders of your relationship. You can also enforce the separation in the physical world by getting rid of reminders of the relationship that still remain in your home or car. These items are like ghosts continuing to haunt your life. If you still have old sweatshirts, return them. Donate or throw away any objects that make you think of them to the point that you can't separate the two in your mind. Get rid of these constant reminders so you can finally stop denying that the relationship is well and truly over.

Reoccurring Forms of Denial

While denial is most common at the beginning of the grieving process, it can reappear later on in different forms. You may start to accept that the relationship is over, but another type of denial involves misrepresenting the events of the relationship and breakup. Maybe you are too hard on yourself, blaming yourself for things that really weren't your fault. Maybe you're misconstruing the truth in the opposite way, absolving yourself of all guilt and deciding that your ex was simply crazy when you both might have said or done things to hurt each other. Neither type of denial really helps you accept reality, and they can breed resentment that makes it harder to let things go. Don't place so much blame on yourself if it's unwarranted, but don't shy away from the truth of why the relationship broke down. This will help guide your personal development as you begin the healing process.

Anger

Once you've stopped denying the reality of the situation you're in, this doesn't necessarily mean you're ready to accept it. On the contrary, you may still have trouble fully processing your breakup and what that means for your life. This leads many to enter the next mechanism of grief: anger.

Anger may seem like an unusual emotion to be part of the grieving process at first glance. Grief is typically characterised as sadness and regret, so what's there to be angry about? However, if you think about the stereotypical breakup reaction shown in movies and TV shows where a jilted lover yells at their ex, destroys their room, and chops half of their hair off in an effort to physically embody the idea of them being a different person, you know that anger is surprisingly common after a breakup, even if you still hold some lingering love for the person.

Getting angry can actually be more common if you're still deeply attached to your ex. It's easier to let go if you know the love in your relationship faded a while ago and the two of you naturally drifted apart over time. It is not quite so easy to let a relationship end if you feel like the rug was torn out from under you. Your anger may not be as obvious as the aforementioned media depictions, but it can still simmer beneath the surface and make itself known at the least opportune times. Everyone handles their anger a little differently, so you may not even recognise what you're feeling as anger initially. Working to understand yourself better can help you bring your emotional expression under control.

Anger is perfectly natural, but it can also be destructive if you don't learn how to manage it. The problem with anger is that it causes you to act and react in ways that you often come to regret once the heat of the moment has worn off. You might say cruel things to your friends, pointedly avoid spending time with family members, and even be needlessly vindictive towards your ex. You should never repress your feelings, but just because your emotions have validity doesn't mean that it's equally acceptable for you to take your frustration out on everyone around you. When you let anger run away with you, you often hurt those who care about you most; these are people who just want to help you through this challenging time in your life. Let yourself express your anger in more constructive and less harmful ways so you can work through it and eventually let go of these difficult feelings.

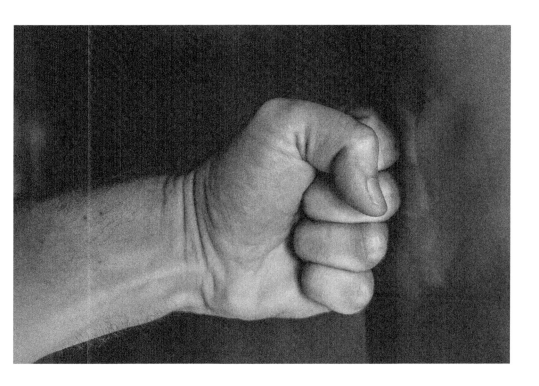

The Dangers of Repressing Anger

Anger can feel like a very counterproductive and harmful emotion. While in some cases it can lead you to do things you wouldn't have done if you were in a better headspace, this doesn't mean anger is all bad, nor does it mean that repression is a healthy tactic for dealing with it. Many people choose to deal with their anger by simply not dealing with it at all, pretending it isn't really there and bottling it up inside them. This is especially common among women, for whom angry outbursts aren't generally seen as socially acceptable. However, these social pressures can be especially damaging because rather than your anger fading away, this repression often only results in anger getting worse over time.

Internalising your anger doesn't help you come to terms with it. One study of women who watched an emotional film and were instructed to either repress or express their anger found that "the women in the study who had suppressed their anger reported feeling more angry, outraged, upset and disgusted," (Graham, 2002, para. 2) even compared to their male counterparts who performed the same exercises. If you don't acknowledge what you're feeling, it continues to linger unaddressed, and you don't get a sense of closure. This can culminate in all of the sudden blowing up at minor problems, since your anger comes not from the immediate issue but instead from all of the prior buildup and repression. When you bottle things up, it's no surprise that eventually the bottle will start to crack.

How to Work Through Your Frustration

If repression isn't a good idea and lashing out can be harmful, then what is the best way to handle the anger stage of grief? According to the same study, strategies that involve substituting your anger by focusing on happier memories and practising gratefulness can be especially effective, at least for women. By directing your thoughts to positive moments in your life or upcoming events that you're excited about, you can alleviate some of the pressure to express your anger in a harmful way. This may be because this allows you to recontextualise the situation and see the bigger picture rather than focusing on the frustrating moment you're currently experiencing. Yes, things are difficult for you now and it's hard to cope, but this doesn't mean you have only ever had negative experiences or that you will always feel this way. Remembering times when you have felt happier can serve as a reminder that better days are ahead and that no emotion lasts forever, not even anger. Over time, the wounds will heal, and your anger will start to fade away.

For men, this kind of mindset shifting may not be quite so beneficial. The study found that male participants "who had substituted angry feelings with a happy memory reported being more upset, outraged and disgusted than did the anger-suppressing males," (Graham, 2002, para. 3) which points to differences in socialisation that affect how men and women are expected to feel and display anger. If the gratitude and positive mindset methods aren't working for you, regardless of your gender, you may find it more helpful to focus on channelling your anger into something constructive so you can express it without harming anyone.

There are many ways to work through your anger that don't involve causing harm to others. Your first instinct may be to lash out, but it's best to let this impulse go and think a little harder about why you feel the way you do. Processing your emotions through careful thought and certain hobbies can alleviate these feelings. In particular, consider hobbies that make you happy, involve physical activity in some way, or encourage you to engage in self-reflection. For example, many people turn to exercise when they're angry. They burn out their anger with a jog around the park or some kickboxing lessons, and by the end of their workout, they feel a little better while also supporting their physical health. However, if you can't stand exercise, this might not be the best method for you. Instead, you could try something like writing, painting, or journaling. These more creative hobbies encourage self-expression. Take what's in your head and lay it all out on the page, expressing your feelings in a way that isn't just completely harmless, but also may help others better understand what you're going through if you choose to share your work. If you're not particularly creative, no worries; this exercise is more about working through your feelings rather than displaying your talent, so it's okay if you aren't exactly Michelangelo. Simply choose a hobby or another constructive activity that allows you to express your emotions in a safe and healthy way, and you will find that with your newfound coping mechanisms, anger is no longer such a significant issue for you.

Understanding Your Anger

The most effective way to handle anger in the long term is to understand why you're angry in the first place, and what specifically is upsetting to you. If you're grieving a lost relationship, your anger comes from your breakup, but this isn't especially specific. Ask yourself questions that shine more light on the issue. Who are you angry at? Are you mad at your ex for breaking things off, or for yourself for not being able to fix the relationship? Are you mad at the world at large and the concept of love, and if so, why? Do you feel like you've been betrayed and misled? What would help these feelings go away? Do you just need time, or are there specific parts of yourself you need to work on before you feel you can improve?

These are tough questions, and they may not have a clear answer at first. Take some time to sit with them before trying to reach a conclusion. Remember that this activity is about better understanding yourself, not just finding an answer and moving on. Use the aforementioned self-reflective hobbies to help you process what you're feeling if you're not sure exactly where these emotions are coming from. Make an effort to get to the bottom of your aggravation, as it is only through true understanding that you can start to heal.

Bargaining

During the bargaining stage, you attempt to fix what went wrong and "go back to normal." You may try to appeal to your ex in an effort to recapture their attention and rekindle the relationship once again. You might promise that you'll be better this time, or that you'll treat them right if you can just start over. You may even try to bargain with God or another higher power to give you a second chance. Bargaining is often a futile effort, as what is done is done, and you cannot go back in time before these issues arose in the first place. Moreover, bargaining can sometimes be dangerous, as it puts you in a position of subservience to your ex if you were to get back together. This can then create a toxic relationship or simply exacerbate the issues that led to the original breakup. While the idea might be appealing thanks to its romanticisation in popular media, more often than not, getting back together with your ex isn't all it's cracked up to be.

The Truth About Rekindling Relationships

Movies make the idea of winning back your ex seem like a fairy tale. They promise that if you can 'fix' what went wrong and make a grand enough gesture that sweeps your ex off their feet, then all prior issues will be resolved and you can forget the whole breakup ever happened. In practice, however, statistics show that this is far from the average experience. In fact, the vast majority of people, once they have worked through their complicated feelings about their breakups, don't end up getting back together or even making much of an attempt to do so.

It's natural to want to rekindle that flame, but research shows that it just doesn't work out this way for most people. Out of a survey of over 3,500 people, all of whom had at one point wanted to restart their relationships with their exes, "the majority of people (70.8%) did not get back together with their ex at all" after the breakup. Of the remaining 29% who did, "about 14% reconciled then broke up again, and about 15% got back together and stayed together" (Dodgson, 2019, para. 18). At this point, you might be saying to yourself, "Maybe I'm part of the 15% then!" While it's true that some couples are able to reconcile their differences, this is a rare outcome, especially if you try to win your ex back right after the end of the relationship. Nerves are too frayed, and feelings are too explosive. When your hurt feelings are right on the surface and no one has had time to grow or change as a person, you're almost certain to experience the same issues that led to breakup all over again, only doubling down on your heartbreak.

Some people overcome this, but it's only by taking time to seriously work on themselves first, and only if their ex-partners choose to do the same.

In short, there's a very slim chance of getting back together with your partner successfully, and it's healthier for both of you if you choose to move on and focus on yourself instead. If you spend all your time bemoaning the one that got away, you will miss out on future opportunities for love. You need to spend time away from this person and reevaluate whether or not they should have a place in your life, and you can only do that if you're choosing to focus on yourself. There's no benefit in living your life caught up in the past, especially when you know deep down that things have changed for both of you since you initially got together.

Accepting Change

Getting through the bargaining phase means learning to accept change in all its forms, good and bad. In life, we can only affect the present moment. We can't predict what the future will hold for us, and we can't turn back time and change the past. Therefore, we cannot truly avoid change, as much as we might try to resist it.

Being hesitant to embrace change is very common because we tend to get set in our ways. We get used to being in a relationship, and we learn to live with any frustrations or other sources of discomfort this causes us, up until they become too much to bear. We might resist ending a relationship simply because we are afraid of the changes it will bring to our lives. After a breakup, everything feels new and different for a while as you get used to navigating the world while single. Things you once did with your partner leave you feeling off-kilter when you have to do them alone. Plans you made for the future now have to shift. You can run from this change, deny it, or try to bargain with life to return things back to the way they were, but all these reactions do is prevent you from moving on. The past is in the past, and you cannot return to it, as much as you might want to. The only way to really move forwards with your life is to accept that things have changed and react to these changes accordingly. This will allow you to let go of your attempts to bargain your way back to the past and help you refocus yourself on the present moment and your bright future.

Depression

Depression typically occurs when you start to let go of your denial and desire to bargain, finally acknowledging the truth of the situation. However, just because you have acknowledged it doesn't mean you are fully comfortable with it yet, nor does this mean you're ready to accept it and move on. Instead, this kind of acknowledgement is more fatalistic. You know that you broke up with your partner and you're not getting back together anytime soon, but you cannot yet envision a positive future coming from this reality. Instead, you find yourself sinking into depression, often entertaining negative thoughts and self-criticisms that you might not have to deal with if you were in a better state of mind.

It's important to note that the depression stage of grief is not quite the same as the psychological condition of depression. While both can negatively impact your mental health, depression as a condition tends to be chronic, often occurring or reappearing without a specific cause and requiring management for anywhere from a few months to multiple years. Depression as a stage of grief, on the other hand, is more of an emotional state, just like anger. It is generally directly tied to your breakup, and it does not typically persist after you've come to terms with the end of your relationship unless you also have underlying mental health issues. In most cases, while this depression can periodically reoccur, its reappearance is connected to thoughts about your past relationship. Therefore, it is a little easier to get these feelings under control without the assistance of medications or therapy, though these can become part of your treatment plan if you've reached a point where you feel you may be a danger to yourself.

Common symptoms of the depression phase of grief include having less enthusiasm about specific events or life as a whole, as well as struggling to drum up motivation to work on important projects. You may be less interested in things that used to bring you joy before. It's also common to have very negative thought patterns. For example, if you're thinking about your breakup, you're more likely to lay the blame at your own feet and berate yourself for not being good enough. If you make a mistake, you may be harsher with your reprimands than you would normally be. It's difficult to handle the loss you're now starting to accept, so you look for someone to blame, even when that someone is yourself. These feelings tend to get even worse if you continue to ruminate in your grief without reaching out to friends and family for support.

Isolation

In addition to issues with your mood, depression can also cause you to isolate yourself, either purposefully or inadvertently. When your enthusiasm suffers, you may withdraw into yourself, leaning into these negative feelings rather than actively trying to improve your mood. You may not feel up to offers to spend time with friends, and you may beg your way out of attending family get-togethers. Rather than giving you space to mentally recover, this often only makes depressive feelings worse. Now, not only have you broken up with your romantic partner, but you've also separated yourself from your entire support network, only reinforcing how alone you feel.

It can be difficult to push through the fatigue and be a little more social, but if you do, it will work wonders for lessening feelings of depression. Whether you're more extroverted or introverted, everyone needs to socialise on a regular basis. You don't have to run out to a big party right away, but just calling a friend when you feel low can help lift your spirits significantly. If you want to stay inside, you can also consider inviting someone over for a cosy day of watching movies or playing games. Otherwise, getting some fresh air by going on a walk with a friend can work wonders. In any case, resist the temptation to cut off your contact with others, and accept the support of your loved ones when you need it most.

Engaging in Positive Thought Exercises

Feelings of depression tend to feed into themselves because you end up stuck in a cycle of negative thoughts. You don't feel up to completing your usual duties, so you put yourself down. You feel worse after you berate yourself, which makes it even harder to stay motivated. Then you say even crueller things to yourself, and this cycle continues until you're so wrapped up in negativity that you don't know how to escape it anymore.

It can be very difficult to break this cycle, but injecting a little positivity and rationalisation can help you interrupt it and get yourself back on the right track. For example, if you notice that you're putting yourself down, pause and evaluate whether you're being fair to yourself. Is it really all your fault that you're all alone, or were there missteps by both you and your ex? Are you really a horrible person for leaving a bad relationship, or did you simply make the best possible choice for your own wellbeing? Try to assess these issues rationally and avoid jumping to the worst possible assumption, as all this does is make you feel worse without giving you an opportunity to improve.

Treat yourself with the same kindness and fairness you would treat one of your friends if they were in your position. Try to be understanding of where you're at right now, and make gradual positive changes whenever you can to shake up your schedule and reconnect with your social circle. Over time, you'll train yourself out of negative thought cycles. As a result, you'll start moving out of the depression phase of grief and onto the final phase, acceptance.

Acceptance

Acceptance is considered the last stage of grief because it is only through fully processing your emotions from the other stages that you can achieve it. In order to accept your situation, you must come to terms with what happened and feel prepared to start looking towards the future. This means you've let go of your denial, learnt how to appropriately express your anger, stopped attempting to bargain with your ex or the universe at large, and eased any feelings of depression the loss created. In short, you understand and come to grips with the breakup, even if you still feel some sadness or regret.

Acceptance is a difficult phase because everyone achieves and experiences it a little differently. It is the most difficult phase to reach as it often takes some hard work and self-reflection first, but it is necessary to learn to accept your breakup before you can start making bigger changes in your life. When you begin to truly accept the way your life is different now, you can learn to let go of the worry, fear, frustration, and distress you feel over your old relationship and begin a new chapter of your life with a fresh start.

Misconceptions About Acceptance

Despite how straightforward it may seem on the surface, acceptance is one of the most commonly misunderstood phases of grief. The biggest misconception is that achieving acceptance means that you are no longer grieving, and that every bit of sadness you previously experienced just falls away. Whether you're grieving over a lost life or a lost relationship, this simply isn't true. In truth, it is very difficult to "get over" anything. You can feel a little better about what happened and know that the breakup ended up being for the best, but this might not mean you're entirely over it. Instead, the acceptance phase simply means you're ready to move on and start looking forwards rather than always looking behind yourself. Some lingering sadness doesn't mean you're engaging in unhealthy behaviours. It just means you're still processing what happened and working towards looking on the bright side, which isn't a bad thing.

Another important point to keep in mind is that acceptance often isn't a permanent mental state. You may feel like you've fully accepted the situation, only for doubt, depression, and anger to flood back in. This is perfectly normal, and it isn't evidence that you're a failure or anything else that your self-deprecating thoughts might tell you. Instead, it simply means you're human like everyone else, and you have good days and bad days. It is natural to have moments of uncertainty, but the more work you put into personal development and growth after a breakup, the easier it will be to shake off these negative feelings and return to the acceptance phase.

Tips on how to get Through the Grieving Process

As you experience some or all of the five stages of grief, you'll likely feel lost and confused. This initial period after a breakup is often the most distressing, as you're highly emotionally vulnerable. You're more likely to make poor snap decisions, and you can engage in some self-destructive behaviours if you don't learn how to manage your emotional expression during this time. To ease the process, there are a few ways you can help yourself endure these trials and get back on your feet.

First, practise accepting the present moment, whatever it may be. Maybe you had a bad day where everything seemed to go wrong, which has brought all your worries to the surface. Maybe you had a good day, but you're sabotaging your own happiness by feeling guilty over your good mood. No matter what happens, your mind can put a negative spin on it or get carried away with stress and anxiety if you let it. Take in new information and try to accept it without letting yourself constantly look on the negative side.

Next, allow yourself to experience your emotions. Resist the urge to force them down and pretend you're perfectly fine. It's good to have a positive outlook, but this doesn't mean you have to ignore any feelings of anger or distress. Give yourself a license to sit with your emotions and to express them in ways that don't harm anyone.

Remember that your goal throughout the grieving process is to learn to move on from your breakup. Avoid constant reminders of the past, and try to be open to the idea of leaving your grief behind. It can be hard to let go of something that was once such an important part of your life, but you cannot heal until you learn to do just that.

If you're struggling with low energy and enthusiasm, try creating and sticking to a regular routine. It's normal to struggle to focus on tasks when you're grieving, and you may have to fend off a strong desire to just crawl back into bed. Creating a routine for yourself encourages you to continue getting up, getting ready for the day, and taking care of everything on your plate, even when you're struggling. This will also ensure you continue to take care of your physical health, as you can make healthy eating and exercise part of your routine.

After a breakup, you may have the sudden desire to radically change your life. Maybe this means buying a new car, quitting your job, or even giving yourself an impromptu haircut. These big changes seem like they're helping you separate yourself from your old life, but they can actually be self-destructive if you don't stop to think through their consequences first. Once the heat of the moment wears off, you're left with expensive monthly car payments, no financial security, and hair that's going to take a few weeks to grow back in. Wait until you can rationally consider these kinds of changes from a place of inner peace so you don't end up making a big mistake.

It might be hard to convince yourself of this, but it's okay to put yourself first after a breakup. If your ex says they need to meet with you again to feel closure but hearing them ask you to take them back would only make things harder for you, don't feel guilty over refusing their request. If you need to take some time off to rest and come to terms with things, let yourself take a much-needed break. Along the same lines, take care of yourself, and pay attention to the wants and needs you may be ignoring. Show yourself kindness and make sure you aren't pushing yourself too hard. You will have good days and bad days; accept the bad ones and move past them so you can make it to the good ones.

While you want to avoid laying unrealistic blame upon yourself after a breakup, it's still important to recognise any mistakes you may have made that contributed to the end of the relationship. Ask yourself whether your expectations for the relationship were realistic, and if you misread any warning signs that could help you avoid a toxic relationship in the future. Think about what you have learnt from this experience that can help you better navigate future relationships. One common complication is getting into a relationship for the wrong reasons. If you start relationships "because someone makes you feel complete, or you believe there's no one else but this person for you, or you're incredibly dependent upon this person, that's simply not good enough or healthy enough" (Brenner, 2019, para. 17) and you'll likely only end up in another relationship that doesn't work out. Take time to self-reflect and determine what you want or need so you can ensure your next relationship is a healthy, equal partnership.

As a final tip, avoid letting yourself indulge in coping mechanisms that just aren't good for you. These can come in a variety of forms, from eating junk food when you feel upset to purposefully reminding yourself of your past trauma to re-open old wounds. Using harmful coping mechanisms is often worse than not using coping mechanisms at all, but ideally you should try to replace them with healthier ones. Instead of turning to high-fat and high-sugar foods, try doing a hobby you love and that brings you joy naturally. Rather than immersing yourself in traumatic material, distance yourself from it and try talking to friends and family about the issues you're facing. The more you utilise these healthier coping mechanisms, the easier it will be for you to heal and keep moving forward.

Grief is never easy to deal with, whether it comes from a breakup or any other type of loss. If you want to feel better, you must make an effort to process what you're feeling first. It is only by coming to terms with your grief that you can begin to set it aside and move on to true mental and emotional healing.

Chapter 4: Introduction to the "FCP Tripod Method"

So far, we've examined the many ways that grief over a breakup can interfere with your life. Now, we'll shift focus and look at strategies that will help you start to move on, allowing you to turn the experience of a breakup into an event with a positive impact on your life. If you only ever recognise the hurt and pain caused by a breakup, viewing it as the end of an era, you're going to see the experience as a net negative no matter how many years pass. This makes it more difficult to fully move on, as you're always harbouring some regret over the end of the relationship. However, when you set your sights on self-development and an effort to work towards a brighter future, you'll find it becomes easier to see the breakup as a necessity and maybe even a net positive in your life.

A breakup isn't just the end of an era of your life. It's also the beginning of a whole new era, and you have the opportunity to make this one even better than the last. This is something I had trouble accepting when my marriage with Roberto ended. Even though I knew the relationship had become toxic and needed to end, it was hard to take those first few steps forward. I felt like I was leaving a part of myself behind, and I wanted to run back to Roberto despite the issues we had, and despite knowing how bad it would be for me to give up on all the progress I had already made. I wasn't sure what to do with myself after the divorce, which left me feeling adrift with no clear goals.

My uncertainty led me to delve deeper into my studies of the human mind, looking for some guidance and a way to ground myself. I found this in the form of my newfound drive for self-discovery and self-improvement. I knew I was lacking in focus, control, and purpose, which had all been in short supply ever since the breakup. To regain these core values and set myself back on the right path, I developed the FCP or tripod method. Focus, control, and purpose make up the three legs of the tripod, which provide support for you as you come out of a relationship and enter into the next period of your life. It is this method that I want to share with you, so you can work to rebuild and rediscover yourself as an individual.

The Three Legs of the FCP Tripod Method

How important are focus, control, and purpose really? When you're recovering from a breakup and learning to get over your last relationship, they're much more integral to your ability to grow and heal than you might think. This is because each of these three qualities are negatively impacted by both a difficult relationship and a breakup.

First, let's take a look at what each of these qualities means in relation to your current situation. Then, in later chapters, we'll look at how you can work to cultivate them and use these traits as tools to overcome your heartbreak.

Focus

Focus refers to your ability to be in the present moment. It means being able to concentrate on the task at hand without being distracted by thoughts of your past regrets or worries for your future. As you might imagine, this runs counter to how people typically feel after a breakup. You're thinking about your history and your old relationship almost constantly, regretting your actions and wishing you could go back, or reflecting on what went wrong and blaming yourself for every issue. Every time you look back to the past, you invite sadness into the present. You start to fear what your future will look like, imagining yourself lonely and old, never finding love again. You forget all the sources of positivity and light in your life, and you remember only the things that help to bring you down. You cannot maintain your focus on the present because you are continually distracted by thoughts of the past and future that have been tinged by a negative mentality, neither of which do much to help you heal.

While setting goals and looking towards the future can be an important part of your healing process, and coming to terms with the past is equally integral, these kinds of thoughts can also be harmful distractions. They can hold you back and prevent you from focusing on your current development. You must be able to engage with the past and present on your own terms and without losing yourself to regret and misery. It is okay to think about all your previous life experiences and what you want for yourself in your future, but these thoughts shouldn't forcefully pull your attention away from looking after yourself in the present.

Improving your focus allows you to use the present moment to better accept the past and plan out your future. It also enables you to exert better control over how you express your emotions. It's very easy to get stuck in a thought spiral where you remind yourself of failure after failure, or where you worry so much about your future that it holds you back from working on basic daily tasks. If your thoughts remain tied to the past, you're going to experience a great deal of bitterness, regret, shame, guilt, and anger that can quickly get out of control. These can lead to mood swings and outbursts, continually re-opening wounds and interfering with your ability to cope with your present circumstances. Through cultivating focus, you'll learn how to gently dismiss these thoughts that fixate on the past and inspire fear about the future, redirecting yourself to the present moment. Focus is all about learning to accept and live the life you have right now, no matter where it takes you.

Control

Focusing on the present can help you mentally prepare yourself to deal with different tasks demanding your attention, but a lack of control can make it challenging to actually complete these tasks. Control involves self-confidence and your willingness to acknowledge your own capabilities. If you believe you can improve yourself and you're ready to take the necessary steps to do so, you will absolutely achieve your goals. On the other hand, if you don't have faith in yourself, you'll find it difficult to keep bad habits under control, which can lead to the development of maladaptive coping mechanisms.

Not every behaviour you take to ease the pain of a breakup is a healthy one. For example, compulsively looking at your ex's pictures on Facebook can greatly interfere with your ability to let them go and move on. You don't feel like you are capable of letting them go, so you continue to engage in these bad habits. Other harmful coping mechanisms can be even more self-destructive. You might turn to drinking, smoking, or partying to dull the ache of your loss, which negatively impacts both your mental and physical health. Other types of dangerous coping mechanisms include binge eating and other forms of disordered eating, persistent self-criticism, engaging in risk-taking behaviours, and getting into fights, both verbally and physically. Once you turn these coping mechanisms into habits, you give them power over you, and you lose control of your own thoughts and actions.

Harmful coping mechanisms are so difficult to break because, on some level, you don't believe you can make it through the day without them. You doubt your own abilities and your mental resilience, which leads you to rely on these dangerous behaviours even against your better judgement. You worry that you're not strong enough to handle things on your own, so you give control over to another force in your life, even if that force is harmful. You may be at a higher risk of engaging in these kinds of coping mechanisms if you're used to your ex-partner being controlling of you, especially if you were in an abusive relationship. This sudden lack of control leaves you adrift, unsure of yourself and potentially unwilling to fully take charge of your life again. However, it is unhealthy to give up your sense of self-control either during or after a relationship, and maladaptive strategies for coping only make it harder for you to heal.

Control is a key tenet of the FCP tripod method because it allows you to rid your life of these harmful habits and replace them with more beneficial ones. It is up to you to control the direction of your life from this moment on. You can work to heal and grow, but you must first believe in your ability to do so. As you develop your self-confidence, you'll be better equipped to work towards self-improvement, and you'll leave the harmful behaviours behind.

Purpose

The final part of the FCP tripod is rediscovering a sense of purpose. This has to do with your personal and professional goals, as well as how they relate to how you engage with each day. Consider whether your behaviours are purposeful and if they're helping you accomplish goals that are important to you, or if they're only serving to hold you back.

You don't want to live your life on auto-pilot. Every task you engage in and every movement you make should serve a greater purpose. This will help motivate you to take care of yourself and maintain your focus and control, even on bad days. Reframe your actions in the context of what you want to achieve. Finding a sense of purpose means recognising that laying on the couch feeling sorry for yourself isn't helping you cope in a healthy way, nor is it assisting you in achieving your other goals in life. As you start to shift your focus to more purposeful behaviours, you'll rediscover a sense of passion and enthusiasm for future relationships and your life as a whole, which will help you embrace a more positive mentality.

In each of the next three chapters, we'll take a look at one of these traits in greater detail. You'll learn how to shift your focus to the present moment rather than lingering in the past. You'll regain your sense of control over both yourself and your life as a whole. You'll rediscover your purpose and choose how you want to work towards fulfilling it. With each leg of the tripod you prop up, you give yourself the support you need to feel fully engaged with your life again. You can stop looking backwards and direct your thoughts towards where you're going to go from here. In short, you will learn how to get over your breakup for good so you can find happiness and hope in your life once again.

Chapter 5: Focus

In my work as a therapist, I've spoken to countless people who have experienced issues with their ability to focus after a bad breakup. One such client had such significant issues with focus that it started to impact her ability to live her life how she wanted to. She was unable to shift her thoughts away from her previous relationship, and it was preventing her from embracing the present in a meaningful way. Rather than looking forwards to new opportunities to find love again, she shied away from any potential partnerships, afraid these would end in explosive breakups too. She couldn't let go of negative self-talk that convinced her she wasn't good enough and she would only ruin any relationship she touched. Her regrets and stress turned into severe anxiety that followed her everywhere she went, souring her mood and causing her to see the world through a negative lens.

Persistent regrets also made it difficult for my client to maintain her physical health. This was most apparent in her inability to fall asleep. Every time she would lay down and try to turn off her brain, she was bombarded by memories that emphasised her greatest failures and downplayed her strengths. She could only think about everything she believed she had done wrong during her relationship and how it had contributed to the breakup, and she was unable to quiet these thoughts for hours on end as they buzzed in her head, keeping her awake well into the night. Unable to clear her mind, she fell asleep late and woke up groggy, which only worsened her mood and made it harder for her to take care of herself. She also found that she tended to reach for junk food more often, trying to artificially raise her mood with caffeine and desserts that did nothing to address the underlying inability to focus that was holding her back.

My client's thoughts of the past became a major distraction that interfered with her ability to accomplish basic tasks. At her job, she was often suddenly beset by bouts of sadness that forced her to put down her task and try to calm herself down before she could return to work. At home, she found her patience for dealing with minor inconveniences frayed, and daily chores weren't being completed because she couldn't work up the motivation. Even previously fun things like watching her favourite shows seemed to struggle to hold her attention, as her thoughts were continually occupied by ruminations on the past and worries about the future. In short, she was unable to focus on just about anything, which meant she couldn't move forward.

Cultivating the ability to focus is an incredibly vital skill after a breakup, when distracting and self-defeating thoughts are often at their loudest. I worked with my client to help her develop strategies that would sharpen her focus and allow her to remain in the present rather than getting lost in the past or future, which are the same strategies I will share with you in this chapter. As a result of adopting these techniques, she was able to improve her concentration and banish distracting thoughts. She regained her sense of motivation for her work and private life, and she started to let go of some of the doubts and regrets that were tethering her to the past. It was a truly transformative experience, as a greater sense of focus let her change her perspective on her life, and create change in her life accordingly.

Focus is a value I strongly believe everyone should learn, which is why it is the first step in the FCP tripod method. Just like my client learnt to harness her focus to reshape her life, you can do the same, as long as you know how to cultivate and direct your focus. This will establish the foundational principle for the rest of the FCP method and make the other legs of the tripod easier to accomplish. When you can focus, you'll find it easier to exert self-control and to curb harmful habits. You'll also find that even though you are bringing your thoughts back to the present when they start to drift, this allows you to plan for the future without getting swept up in endless worries, so you can start to connect with your newfound sense of purpose. Focusing on the present really is an invaluable tool, and it can help you manage and overcome the emotional turmoil that comes from the end of a relationship.

What Does it Mean to Focus?

In a general sense, focusing refers to your ability to concentrate and to resist the temptation of distractions. When applied to the context of a breakup, the term takes on a slightly different meaning. Namely, it refers to the idea of spending less time thinking about the past and future, and spending more time in the present. This allows you to work through your current emotions and quell any distress that comes from rumination and worry. Focus lets you calm your anxieties and work towards making improvements in the present moment, which can completely reshape your mindset.

It may not be immediately clear how damaging the act of constantly thinking of the past and future can be. This may seem like a relatively harmless habit, but the damage it can do to your outlook on life is significant. It's important to recognise these dangers so you can avoid them through strategies that allow you to recenter yourself.

How Rumination can Sabotage you

Rumination refers to the habit of repeatedly fixating on the same thoughts, which are usually self-critical or self-deprecating. When you ruminate after a relationship, you tend to think about the loss of the relationship, as well as important moments that stand out in your mind. However, this is rarely a fair and unbiased way of thinking about the relationship. Instead, you may find yourself ruminating on all the worst moments. You might remember the arguments, full of fear and anger, that only became more frequent and intense as the relationship progressed. You might remember all the cruel things your ex said about you and start to internalise these ideas. You might remember feeling hopeless and unloved, and over time these kinds of ruminations can convince you that you are to blame for all the hardships in your life. This can exacerbate feelings of depression and make it harder to engage with the present moment, as you can't seem to escape your past.

Alternatively, you may think only of the good times, and in doing so, convince yourself that you've lost the best thing that has ever or will ever happen to you. It is easy to see past relationships through rose coloured glasses. You focus only on the best moments and ignore all the times when the relationship was strained. By looking at your past through this lens, it's hard to move on because you've idealised this moment in time so much. You know you can never return to the past, but you can't manage to focus on the present because the harsh reality of your current situation seems so much worse than the idealistic picture of the past you created in your mind. You miss your relationship so strongly that you can't imagine moving on from it, which keeps you stuck in the past.

The truth is that your life doesn't end with the end of your relationship, no matter how good or bad that relationship might have been. Your mind tricks you into only remembering the very good and very bad moments, when in reality, there were so many more events that played into the way things ended between you and your ex. You might have had good times and bad times; this doesn't mean you will never experience joy and love again, nor does it mean that you are unworthy of happiness in your future. When you ruminate, you forget to pay attention to what you're doing right now and where you want to go from here, and you allow doubt and regret to take over your worldview.

How Worry Can Sabotage You

Much like rumination, worry is another source of persistent stress and anxiety. Where rumination deals with the past, worry is primarily produced by uncertainty about the future. For example, now that your relationship is over, you might not know where your life will go from here. How do you move on as a newly single person? What do you do now that you're on your own and you're not sure what comes next? What if the future only holds more heartbreak and loneliness? These kinds of questions can be so frightening that they lead you into a seemingly endless spiral of worry and doubt.

The period after a breakup is an especially uncertain time in your life, so it's only natural to be apprehensive. However, when these reasonable nerves turn into paralysing anxiety, they can keep you from taking things one day at a time. If you get so caught up in fears about your future that you can't bring yourself to focus on much at all right now, you're essentially sabotaging your own potential. Your future is continually changing based on the choices you make in the present moment. If you choose to do nothing, or if you make harmful choices that distract you from your goals, you only allow your fears about the future to take root, setting the stage for them to eventually come true. In this way, you create a self-fulfilling prophecy. Your constant worry prevents you from taking action, and this lack of action leads you towards exactly the outcomes you most feared.

One especially common worry that occurs after a breakup is a fear of future relationships. Your last relationship ended badly, so you might assume that your next relationship will end this way as well. This can cause you to avoid putting yourself out there again since you don't want to be hurt a second time. You might withdraw from social situations, cutting off your ability to form new platonic and romantic relationships and straining the bonds of your current ones. This doesn't do you any favours, as it only works to confirm your worst fears that all your relationships will end in unhappiness. While no relationship is guaranteed to last forever, this also means that no relationship is guaranteed to end in failure either. You don't know until you try, and trying means opening yourself up to the possibility of love even if there's a risk of being hurt. If you allow your worries to get in your way, you'll never know if you're missing out on a potential partnership, and you'll struggle to move forwards with your life.

At this point, you should have a good idea of why distracting thoughts that pull your focus to your past and future can be harmful. This only emphasises how important it is to develop your ability to maintain your focus on the present moment. When you can let go of your worries and calmly return your thoughts to the present, you can focus less on your anxieties and regrets, and more on taking action to stabilise your emotions and create positive change.

Methods for Improving Focus

It's easy to get carried away with your thoughts if you aren't making a dedicated effort to remain focused. To avoid this, it's important to have methods for refocusing yourself when you need them. There are a variety of ways you can accomplish this, and what works for one person might not work for others. You might find success in meditation and other mindfulness-based practices that help to calm the mind, or you may find it more beneficial to simply choose a task and work on it a certain way. Whatever method you use should help you sharpen your concentration, boost your motivation, and complete various tasks, even on your worst days. These include establishing routines, practising self-care, refocusing on your priorities, and restructuring your environment.

Establishing Routines

Humans are habitual creatures by our nature. When we create and stick to routines, we're more likely to engage in positive behaviours on a routine basis. Habits are so prevalent that "studies by neurobiologists, cognitive psychologists, and others indicate that from 40 to 95 percent of human behaviour—how we think, what we say, and our overall actions—falls into the habit category" (Walesh, n.d., para. 2). We tend to continue doing the things we do all the time, and we're hesitant to break our routines in favour of trying something new. Our habitual nature can work for us or against us, depending on what kinds of routines and habits we embrace.

Habits must be purposefully created to be of any help to you. If you allow yourself to fall into harmful patterns and turn negative coping mechanisms into habits, you'll have a hard time ridding yourself of their influence. On the other hand, if you take time to create routines that block out periods of time for completing various tasks, you'll have an easier time remaining focused as these routines become habitual. Taking charge of your daily schedule is just one step in improving your concentration skills and productivity, but it's an important one that can help to put you in the right mindset for getting things done.

Keep in mind that a breakup represents a drastic shift in your usual routines. For example, you might be used to sitting down to dinner every night at the same time with someone else, and now that you're cooking for one, it can be hard to continue keeping up with your nutritional needs. You may be tempted to order out or binge on junk food routinely instead. This habit develops unintentionally, so even though it is causing you harm, you don't consciously notice this until the habit has been ingrained in your regular routines. Bad habits can make themselves known in all sorts of areas of your life, not just in what you eat. This is why it is so important to create routines that support your health and happiness, and that encourage you to focus on the present moment rather than lingering in sadness over the past. Turning healthy habits into just another part of your daily routine not only improves your focus, but also helps to keep you grounded when your thoughts threaten to overwhelm you.

When establishing new routines, start small and work your way up to bigger changes. If you want to start a routine of focusing on your work at a certain time, you can build up your focus in five-minute increments. Tell yourself you're going to work on a project for five minutes without letting your thoughts return to rumination or worry. Then, do your best to follow through on your promise. If you notice your thoughts drifting, pause, recenter yourself, and restart the timer as you return to your work. With a few tries, you should be able to maintain your focus for this brief period of time. From there, you can keep expanding the habit, aiming for 10 or 15 minutes of uninterrupted work, and then even longer. Try to start your work at the same time each day, so you mentally prepare yourself for it before you even sit down at your desk. Before long, working at this time will come naturally to you, and it will be much easier to push aside distracting thoughts so you can focus on what you need to do.

Practising Self-Care

Regular self-care is important at any time, but especially when you're under the amount of stress you're experiencing right now. You're more likely to experience more intense bouts of anxiety, frustration, self-doubt, and depression when you're feeling physically and mentally worn down. Going through a breakup is tough, and it's important that you give yourself an appropriate amount of time to heal. Constantly pushing yourself isn't going to do you any favours. Instead, it will just make the exhaustion worse, and it will allow self-doubts and regrets to creep into your mind on a regular basis.

Resting and relaxing when you're at your limit is absolutely vital. It can be tough to give yourself permission to slow down because you might feel like if you stop flitting from one task to another, your thoughts will return to rumination. In these cases, you can try combining relaxing activities with thoughts exercises meant to help you relax and clear your mind. For example, many people use yoga as a stress reliever. The exercise keeps you moving and supports your physical health, and you get a mental workout at the same time. Yoga mantras help to keep your mind in the present moment, and the exercises ensure you remain grounded. Of course, exercise isn't for everyone, and there are plenty of other ways you can restore your mind and body. You could try out a guided meditation while taking a bath, or you could work through your thoughts by writing them down in a journal. Find a method that helps you feel more well-rested and ready to face the challenges of the day.

While self-care is important, you should avoid overindulging, or using unhealthy behaviours as your form of self-care. Eating sweets might make you feel better for a moment, but it doesn't actually leave you well-rested or more at peace with yourself, and it can have a negative effect on your health in the long run if you develop a dependency on sugar to keep you going. Instead, turn to activities that are good for your mind, body, and soul. These will have the most significant effects on your mindset and encourage more long-term positive change.

Refocusing on Your Priorities

Disorganised priorities can be a significant hurdle when you're trying to focus. You might put off starting an important but difficult project so you can work on something that's not particularly urgent just because you're struggling to focus on the more difficult task. While this might seem like a momentary stress reliever, this only means you'll have to work hard to make up for lost time when you finally do get around to tackling the neglected task. This can inspire even greater levels of stress and anxiety, reinforcing the negative thoughts in your head and making it nearly impossible to focus on the task.

You can eliminate many of these anxieties by simply adjusting your priorities. Consider which tasks are important and time-sensitive, and which might be wasting time that could be better spent elsewhere. Additionally, think about why you're accomplishing each task. Maybe you don't want to work on a difficult project, but if it helps you accomplish an important personal goal, then it should still be a high priority for you. Recognising this can help you find the motivation to deal with these tough tasks without the stress that typically comes with them.

If you run into trouble, remember that the only way to complete a task is to actually start it. Just taking the first step, no matter how small, can encourage you to keep going until you've made significant progress. If you're struggling to feel comfortable socialising again after a breakup, start with a single conversation with a close friend. If you need to focus on your work, try putting down all distractions and working on the task at hand for just a few minutes. In most cases, your momentum will carry you through, and you'll be able to tackle these priorities head-on with your full focus.

Restructuring Your Environment

Your surroundings have a significant impact on your behaviours, even though you might not recognise their influence. Think about trying to accomplish a task that requires a lot of dedicated focus, such as reading a book. If you're sitting on the living room couch with the TV playing in the background and your phone constantly lighting up with notifications, you're going to keep getting interrupted. Your attention will waver and you'll find it more difficult to get fully immersed in whatever you're reading. You might find yourself rereading entire paragraphs because you reached the end only to realise you don't remember what you just read. With so many distractions, it's impossible to hear your own thoughts, let alone to focus on the thoughts of someone else.

Making adjustments to your environment so your surroundings are conducive to the task at hand can help you avoid these annoying, distracting thoughts. Try to surround yourself with only the things you need to complete your work. Clear away clutter that can create a lot of visual noise. Just moving things out of your line of sight can significantly restrict their ability to distract you. To return to the previous example, you might find it easier to focus on your book if you move to a part of your house that is quiet and helps you feel more at peace. Curl up in a comfy chair with a pile of blankets, and make sure your surroundings are well-lit. Even just getting up to turn off the TV and put your phone on silent can help you block out any interruptions that pull your attention away from your task. The more you shape your surroundings to suit your needs and promote peace and concentration, the less time you'll waste.

Even when you're not trying to accomplish a specific task, your environment can still help or hinder your efforts—especially when it comes to healing after a breakup. It's a lot harder to stop thinking about an ex when you still have their sweatshirt draped over the back of a chair in your bedroom, or when you listen to music that reminds you of them. You don't have to give up all of your interests just because they have some form of connection to your ex, but it's a good idea to remove these reminders from your surroundings until you're better equipped to handle them. Otherwise, you will find that they serve as especially effective distractions.

Digital spaces should follow the same rules. Unfriend and unfollow your ex's social media accounts to give yourself a clean break. You may want to limit how much time you spend on sites that remind you of them as well if you need to. Remember that you get to choose where you spend your time when you go on any website. You can decide to be productive and consume content that makes you feel better, or you can seek out content that reminds you of past mistakes and worsens your anxiety about the future. It is up to you to craft a more positive and productive environment that lets you focus on the present.

No matter what method you use to improve your focus, remember that this is just the first step towards recovering after a breakup. Sharpening your focus lets you take life one day at a time, quieting the loudest negative thoughts and helping to reaffirm your belief in your own capabilities. This will make it much easier for you to slowly but surely regain a sense of control during an otherwise turbulent time in your life.

Chapter 6: Control

In Chapter 1, we discussed how one common sensation after a breakup is a loss of security. You're used to living your life a certain way and feeling confident in your ability to maintain this lifestyle. A breakup serves to shatter this illusion, or at least, that is how it appears on the surface. Rather than reaffirming your own sense of self-assurance, a breakup leaves you lost and confused, no longer sure of your own abilities. After all, you might tell yourself, you weren't able to keep your ex happy like you thought you could. Does this mean you're going to fail at your other tasks too? How can you still feel like you're in control of your own life if you cannot believe in yourself?

These kinds of questions can leave you completely shaken, which is why it is so important to regain your sense of security after a breakup by restoring your control. Even though you might not recognise it right now, you do have the ability to shape your life for better or for worse. You might not be able to control what others say and do, but you always have control over one thing: your mind. You can choose how you want to react to any given situation. If you learn to look for the silver lining to even the darkest of clouds, you will find that these clouds don't bother you so much anymore. After all, this is exactly what you're doing now by turning your breakup into an opportunity to develop as a person. You can't go back in time and prevent the breakup, nor can you control the actions of your ex. But you can control what you choose to do with your life now that your fate is in your hands once again. This starts with developing your self-confidence.

Competence and Control

Many people misunderstand the idea of 'control' as trying to influence the behaviours of others, or trying to directly affect a certain situation. While this kind of control might be useful, it isn't particularly realistic, nor is it exactly what I'm talking about when I refer to control's role in the FCP method. Instead, in this circumstance, control means feeling like you are "in control" of yourself and your life. It means embracing the idea that you are competent and you can handle the challenges you're facing in your life right now.

This belief is often undermined after a breakup because you are so full of doubt, fear, and regret. You worry that you won't be able to handle all the challenges you're facing and you start to doubt your capabilities on a fundamental level. This extends far past worrying you won't be able to maintain a relationship, working to convince you that you aren't as competent as you thought you were in all sorts of areas. For example, you might undermine your success at your job because you pass up opportunities to take on a new task, worried you might fail.

There's a good chance you could turn to harmful habits as a way to take some of the pressure off your shoulders, which only ends up making the problem worse in the long run. These kinds of coping mechanisms only feed into the negative beliefs you hold about yourself, making it harder to replace bad habits with healthier ones. You might tell yourself you're just not strong enough to cope with your breakup without the use of bad habits, so you don't try to change your behaviour for the better. The longer you persist in engaging with these harmful activities, the harder it becomes to break the habit, all while your self-esteem continues to fall.

Negative self-talk can also have a serious impact on your mental picture of yourself. Everyone has strengths and weaknesses, and it is okay to not initially find success in everything you try. One relationship ending in a breakup doesn't mean you're going to fail at maintaining all future relationships, but this line of thinking can lead you to close yourself off and give up on finding your happy ending, either as an individual or with a new partner. As you continue to think harmful, unfair things about yourself, your self-esteem suffers, which can make it harder to feel like you're in control of your own life.

The Dangers of low Self-Esteem

One of the greatest dangers of low self-esteem is that it leads you to believe that you have little ability to affect the quality of your life. You worry that you can't change who you are for the better, and you fear the idea of other people knowing you on such an intimate level again. You may hide parts of yourself that you fear others might not like, presenting a disingenuous version of yourself. Worse, low self-esteem leads you to view your current problems as permanent issues that you can't do anything to change, when in reality simply adjusting your mindset can make even the worst of situations more tolerable. When you have a negative mindset, you feel like you cannot control your life, and any obstacles you face seem insurmountable.

One reason for this is that you may be going through life trying to avoid failure rather than attempting to pursue success. This affects the relationships you have with others as well as the way you hold mental conversations with yourself. Simply reframing the way you think about what you do every day can change your perception of it. As Virginia Tech psychology professor Scott Geller points out in his TEDx Talk, "You probably told your friends, 'I've got to go to class. It's a requirement.' Not, 'I get to go to class. It's an opportunity" (Geller, 2013). Finding a sense of control in your life is all about looking for opportunities rather than requirements. If you feel like others control what you do and how you spend your time, you will be less receptive to everything you learn, you will have less motivation, and you will have less confidence in your own abilities. If you reframe your thoughts to emphasise the opportunities available to you, you'll improve your self-esteem, rediscover your motivation to put yourself out there and try new things, and truly feel like you're in control of your life. This is self-control, and it's an invaluable part of rediscovering yourself after a breakup or any big change in your life.

Regaining Self-Control

When cultivating control, it's important to focus on control of the self. After all, you are the one thing you always have control over. People can quickly erode their confidence when they try to control other people or the world at large. They wonder why they feel ineffective and uncertain. They want others to act a certain way, or they want the universe to change according to their whims, and they're baffled and hurt when that doesn't happen. You can spend the rest of your life hoping your ex changes their mind and they decide to come back to you, but nothing you do will control what they choose to do. No matter how many pleading texts you send and how many times you might break down into tears wishing things were different, other peoples' actions are their own to decide, just as you get to choose how you respond to your current circumstances. No, you can't control the world, but you can control yourself. In some cases, this is practically the same thing, and self-control will alter the way you view the world.

When you know you are in control of your own actions, you feel more motivated to pursue lofty goals and achieve great feats. You recognise your own ability for change and growth, which empowers you to improve your mindset and express more gratitude for the sources of positivity in your life. You can start to cultivate these feelings of competency and self-control in your life by engaging in activities that showcase your abilities. You might start by engaging in small tasks that help build up your confidence, reminding yourself that you have agency over your life. From there, you can establish reasonable limits about what you can and can't control so you can stop stressing about the things that are outside of your authority and focus on the things you can positively impact: namely, yourself.

Long and complicated tasks can seem overwhelming when you think of all the work that needs to go into them. When you're staring at a blank canvas, it's hard to see how you can turn it into a finished product, and you might get caught up in thinking about all the work you have to do to get there. This is as true for everyday tasks as it is for projects like self-improvement and other methods for turning your life around. You may start to doubt your abilities just because there is so much work ahead of you. You might go, "There's no way I can finish this whole task, so why should I even try in the first place?" This kind of thinking is inherently defeatist. In choosing not to make an attempt, you're handing over control, and you're letting go of any chance you would have had to surprise yourself and succeed.

It can help to recontextualise big projects as just a series of smaller steps that take you from your starting point to your goal. If you can break a big task down into smaller chunks, you'll realise that you're more than capable of completing each of these mini-tasks, which means you really do have the self-control to finish a large project as long as you approach it the right way. As an example, let's look at the task of decluttering a room. If your room is especially messy, you might put off trying to clean up because you know it's going to take a lot of work, and you feel like you're not up to the task. If you're feeling low because you're still dealing with hurt feelings, you may not have the motivation to clean for multiple hours, knowing it will leave you exhausted and you might give up halfway through. This is where breaking the task down can help you re-establish control over any situation, whether it's a messy room or a messy mental state.

Instead of thinking about how difficult the entire task will be, start with something small. Spend five minutes collecting garbage and throwing it away. This is such a small task that there's no excuse to give up on it. At the same time, just five minutes of effort can already make a big difference in how much clutter you have to deal with. As mentioned previously, your environment plays into your mentality. If you straighten up your surroundings, you might start to feel a little more mentally organised with fewer distractions and reminders of your less desirable traits in your environment. Ticking off this five-minute task can give you a mood boost because you know you're making progress on a difficult task. It might inspire you to keep working, and before long you'll realise what started as a five-minute exercise has now resulted in a completely decluttered room. Now, your sense of self-control and your measure of your own capabilities really get a boost, because you've gone above and beyond the goalposts you set for yourself. You can use this method of creating mini-tasks to 'trick' your brain into completing all sorts of tasks, just by starting small and working your way through the project one step at a time. With each mini-task you tick off the list, you remind yourself that you are capable, smart, and strong, and you start to regain your sense of control.

As you develop your self-confidence, you'll be able to take on more and more demanding tasks. Always start with something easily manageable so you can train your tolerance for less enjoyable tasks. Over time, you'll build up your stamina, and you'll find it easier to recognise your own strengths. This helps to push back against negative self-talk and the bad habits it inspires, letting you let go of negativity and live a more peaceful and personally fulfilling life.

Expanding Your Comfort Zone

It's difficult to feel confident about new experiences because you don't have the same level of familiarity with them. You don't know how good you'll be so that you might avoid ever trying in the first place. This can be unfortunate, as it limits you to only doing things you've done before, and forces you to pass up opportunities for improvement and growth. Relying too heavily on your comfort zone can also cause you to shy away from gradually progressing on a task, as discussed in the previous section. You feel comfortable with the small stuff, but how do you keep making progress without feeling like your success is completely out of your control?

It might be frightening to try new things, as it does require you to give up a little bit of your control. You don't know how good you're going to be in this new pursuit, but you'll never find out unless you give it a try. In these situations, remind yourself that failure doesn't have to be such a devastating outcome. It's difficult to leave your comfort zone after a breakup because you're afraid of 'failing' again. However, the only real way any relationship can be considered a failure is if it prevents you from pursuing your own happiness in the future. Every relationship, even the worst ones with the most explosive breakups, teaches you something. You learn how to find compromises with your partner, and you learn where you need to set your boundaries to ensure a relationship remains healthy. You learn how to express your love and what kinds of behaviours to avoid. Even if you don't stay in a relationship with the same person forever, this doesn't mean this period of your life was a waste, nor that the breakup was necessarily a bad thing. If you use it as an opportunity to grow, you'll see that even your greatest 'failures' can actually be positive experiences in another light. This realisation makes it easier to leave your comfort zone behind, try new things, and put yourself out there. You can regain the confidence you felt prior to your breakup, and this confidence will allow you to push back against bad habits, focusing your efforts on opportunities for positive change.

It can be difficult to maintain self-control if you tend to look at the small-scale results of your actions. What something gets you in the short-term might seem more important than its long-term consequences. If you're feeling down, it's easy to slip into bad habits this way. You start regretting your breakup and thinking negatively about yourself, so you reach for a quick fix, like a sugary snack or a cigarette, to help you feel a little better. At the moment, this helps bring your emotions back under control, but it actually results in you giving up control in the long term.

When you engage in bad habits to manage your emotions, you often make yourself dependent on these quick fixes. Whenever you feel a little down in the dumps because you're thinking about your breakup again, you don't attempt to work through these feelings on your own; instead, you do some "retail therapy" with online shopping, or you start procrastinating the work you have to get done. These are harmful habits to adopt, especially because you have now strengthened the connection between feeling upset and performing the habit. You're ignoring the long-term harm that these kinds of bad habits can cause in favour of the short-term gains they provide.

One way to avoid doing this is to consider the future outcome of your actions and whether or not they bring you closer to your personal goals. Is smoking helping you feel happier and supporting your wellbeing, or is it actually bringing you further away from this goal? Does reaching for sugar or caffeine really do anything to improve your mood in the long run, or is it a short-term fix that wears off quickly and isn't worth the harm it does to your health? When you adjust your perspective, you consider where your present actions are leading you, and whether or not this is a path you want to continue to walk. This can be a powerful motivator to quit bad habits and replace them with better ones, allowing you to regain self-control.

Take Care of Yourself

Temptation undermines self-control and self-confidence. The reason why bad habits are so hard to break is that they represent a form of temptation that can be hard to resist when you're struggling to manage your wants and needs. You're more likely to crave something you know you shouldn't have if you're stressed and anxious than you are if you're perfectly content, because you believe the thing you're craving will help alleviate the tension. For example, people often find it difficult to quit smoking not just because of their physical dependence on nicotine, but also their mental dependence on its ability to relax them and help clear their mind of anxiety-ridden thoughts. If you can find alternate ways of managing emotional turmoil, you're less likely to be swayed by temptation, and you'll have an easier time quitting smoking and other bad habits.

Taking care of yourself is crucial if you want to alleviate the power of temptations. This means caring for both your physical and mental health, as they are connected. The better your physical health is, the easier you will find it is to remain mentally strong, and vice versa. When you take care of yourself, engaging in self-care and rest days when you need them while also making healthy choices regarding exercise and diet, you give yourself the mental fortitude you need for greater self-control.

Recognising the Limits of Your Control

While control is important, it has its limitations. You cannot control everything in your life, and you're just going to frustrate yourself if you try to do so. When something is out of your control, you have two options. You can get frustrated and continue trying to change it even though you can't, or you can recognise that it's out of your control and adjust your response to the situation instead.

You cannot control whether or not your ex broke up with you any more than you can turn a rainy day into a sunny one. Other peoples' thoughts and actions are outside the limits of your control. If you keep trying to change their mind, you're only going to anger and upset both of you. At the same time, you can control your reaction to the breakup. You can let yourself wallow in sadness and self-pity indefinitely, only feeling worse as each day passes, or you can work to process your emotions and express them in healthy ways. One option will leave you stuck in misery, while the other will help you move on. It is up to you to decide which outcome you want to pursue, as only you can control your actions after a breakup. Only you can decide if you're ready to start looking inward and embracing a newfound sense of purpose instead.

Chapter 7: Purpose

Purpose is something we must all have in order to find a sense of fulfilment in our lives. It gives us the drive we need to treat every day like an opportunity to learn and grow, which allows us to feel enthusiastic about our present and our future. Despite its importance, many people go through life without considering what their purpose really is. They go through each day on autopilot, completing tasks just because they're part of their schedule and not because they have an overarching goal they're working towards. This can lead many people to feel burnt out and, in some cases, like life isn't worth living, especially after a big event like a breakup. What do you do now that your life has completely changed? How do you find your guiding focus so you can get back on your feet and live your life with determination and purpose again?

Understanding the purpose of your life does not have to involve spending hours meditating atop a mountain or years of self-reflection. In fact, if you can answer a few simple questions, you're off to a good start. In his Tedx Talk, Adam Leipzig suggests that for people who felt like they understood their life's purpose, they knew five things. He lists these as "who they were, what they did, who they did it for, what those people wanted or needed, and what they got out of it—how they changed as a result" (Leipzig, 2013). These are simple questions, but they are the foundational ideas behind discovering what motivates you and what you're passionate about. Discovering a newfound sense of purpose after your breakup is a powerful agent of change in your life. It can take some time to know exactly how you would answer these questions, but as you come to understand what your purpose is, you will start to truly believe that you have value as an individual, not just as someone in a relationship. This will be the last boost you need to move on from your breakup and focus on the incredible life that lies ahead of you.

Understanding Your Purpose

Before you can know exactly what your purpose is, you must first understand what having a purpose really means. This is much more than a single task or goal that you can complete in a matter of days or weeks. It is different from a hobby you start on a whim, and which you may or may not stick with after your initial enthusiasm burns out. Purpose is much more powerful than these fleeting, temporary goals, and it shapes your life in a much more profound way.

For one, your purpose is, in essence, the goal of your life. Depending on your faith, you may believe it is what you were put on this earth to accomplish, or you may take a different view and see it as the culmination of your life's efforts. Your purpose isn't something you can pick up and drop again whenever the mood strikes you. Every decision you make affects your ability to pursue your life's purpose. Additionally, purposes often don't have a specific point that marks the finish line. Most people don't have a set point where they can say they have 'completed' their purpose, which separates them from standard goals. Instead, it is something you continually work towards, and which you come to embody in your thoughts and actions.

At the same time, you don't need to have one unilateral purpose that plays into every single area of your life. You might complete different tasks for different reasons. For example, maybe you work to put food on the table for your family, but you practise your hobbies as a way to work towards more creative goals that you hold close to your heart. You might have a different purpose underlying each task that you do. This is great, as it provides you with motivation to achieve the goals you set out to complete. When you feel like your actions have a greater meaning, they will better hold your attention, and you'll start to truly embrace each day.

Another aspect of discovering your purpose is considering how your actions impact others in your community. Deriving your purpose means thinking beyond yourself. It means recognising that you can enrich others' lives while also improving your own, and making a commitment to doing so. Your purpose is something you do outside of your individual sphere that allows you to positively impact someone else, whether that "someone else" is an individual, a society or a certain environment.

Think again about the five things you need to know to discover your life purpose. The majority of these questions and their answers have to do with your impact on other people. The most introspective of the group is knowing who you are, which requires you to develop a strong sense of self. However, the following responses are all geared around the service you can provide to others. The question of "What do you do?" is really one of, "What do you feel most qualified to teach others?" What kinds of experiences have you had that you believe others would benefit from hearing about? The next topic deals with why you do what you do, but reframes the question to focus on the people you're supporting. These can be people in your family, your friend group, or your wider community of people with shared experiences. Your motivation is then derived from the needs of others, not just your own needs. What do these people want that you can provide? How are you helping to better enrich your community through your existence?

This will help you answer the final question, which has to do with what you get out of the experience of helping others. When you see that you have benefitted someone else, how does it make you feel? Why do you want to help people or show them your point of view?

As you answer each of these questions, you're not really focusing on yourself. You're centring the wants and needs of others, and only considering yourself in relation to your community. Humans are social creatures, and it's often easier and more meaningful for us to help the people we care about rather than help ourselves. If you live a life of service to others, you will be able to look back on your life with pride in your accomplishments. This is the kind of motivation that will help you brave any big life event, because you know there is more for you to do on this earth.

Living Your Life Purposefully

After my divorce, I didn't feel like I had truly recovered and started to move on until I started to discover my own purpose in life. I was out of an unhealthy relationship and well into the next stage of my life, and yet I felt something was missing until I realised that I wanted to help others in their darkest moments, just as my friend had helped me. I wanted to serve as a life coach to those who needed it, which is why I became interested in therapy. At this point, I was no longer living just for myself. I was living for the people I was helping, and they were benefiting from my actions just as much as I was.

Once I understood what made me feel fulfilled, I was able to live each day purposefully. I returned to my studies, even though I had dropped out shortly before getting married, because I knew I needed to graduate to pursue being a therapist. I started paying more attention to my own physical wellbeing and mental state, because I knew I had to be strong in order to serve as a guiding example for others. I rediscovered a sense of passion and peace in my life because I was finally doing something I cared about rather than just going through the motions. I knew my purpose, and each choice I made helped me work towards that purpose. This was an absolutely life-changing way to experience each day, and I firmly believe that if I had never taken the time to find my true calling, I might not be as happy and enthusiastic as I am today. I wouldn't have thought to use my breakup as a growth opportunity, and I wouldn't be the person I am now. Living a purposeful life allowed me to put the focus and control I had cultivated to good use so I could be happier, and so the people around me could be happier as well.

Chapter 8: How to Apply the FCP Method

The FCP method is especially useful because of its versatility. It can be applied to a number of different situations, and each of the three aspects works together to enable you to improve various areas of your life. While the primary goal is to help you break free from the post-breakup slump, the FCP method derives its powerful effects from its ability to help you tackle a number of different problems in your life. These include your decision-making skills, health, diet and exercise, spirituality, hobbies, career, and family.

While addressing each of these areas, it's important to recognise how the different parts of the FCP method support each other. Focus is the most foundational quality, as it helps you shift your thoughts from the past to the present, and makes it possible to plan for the future without getting lost in worries and fears. This allows you to exert greater control over your life because you can focus on the tasks you want to achieve, helping you develop your self-confidence and leave bad habits behind. You then replace these bad habits with better ones that allow you to achieve your purpose, now that you have had the chance to reflect and decide exactly what that purpose will be. Focus and control enable you to live a more purposeful life, and when you have a goal to work towards, you find it easier to control your impulses and maintain your focus on the present moment in turn. Acknowledging the connections between each leg of the FCP tripod will help you understand how you can use each of the aspects together to begin the healing and growing process in different areas of your life.

Decision Making

A lack of focus, control, and purpose can seriously impair your ability to make level-headed decisions. When you're unfocused, your mind is clouded by doubt and anxiety. You can't focus on the present reality of the situation because you're afraid of the possibility of a negative outcome. This can lead you to make poor, impulsive decisions, or lead you to avoid any kind of risk, even if it could be a good opportunity for you. Similar issues arise if you lack control. If you undersell yourself, you'll likely go for the safest bet, which isn't always the best decision. You may be hesitant to take on new projects or even talk to new people because you've convinced yourself you're just going to fail before you've even given yourself the chance to try. Without purpose, you're more likely to make decisions that run counter to your ability to achieve your goals. You may unknowingly sabotage yourself, all because you don't know what you want to achieve, why it matters, and how you should go about working towards it.

The FCP method allows for better decision making because it resolves these issues with focus, control, and purpose. When you build up your focus, you can make a more accurate assessment of the pros and cons of each choice without the interference of worry and fear. As you start to feel more certain in your capabilities, you can make honest judgements about your ability to handle tasks, as well as the limits of your control. When you know your purpose, you can make choices that align with your aspirations and avoid making bad decisions that exchange long-term results for a minor short-term benefit. With the FCP method, you'll find it easier to evaluate your options, decide what you can and can't handle, and make decisions that bring you closer to achieving your goals, which in turn helps you experience a more productive and fulfilling life.

Health

Your physical and mental health are equally important, but these concerns can often end up brushed aside when you're experiencing a lot of emotional turmoil. After a breakup, you may do little to take care of yourself, especially if you experience post-breakup depression that can make it harder to work up the energy to do much of anything. You might put things like personal hygiene on the back burner, and you're more likely to let spiralling negative thoughts interfere with your sleeping habits when you can't focus. There's also a good chance you'll pick up some bad health habits if you can't muster up much self-control during this time, and if you don't act to correct these habits quickly, they can stick around for months or years after your breakup.

If you want to start feeling better after the end of your relationship, you need to take care of yourself, and that starts with maintaining your health. You need the focus to worry about yourself in the present rather than deciding you'll engage in healthy habits only when you feel better; if you let your health deteriorate, it's going to take much longer for you to bring your emotions back under control. You can use this self-control to curb bad habits and replace them with ones that help you get out of your slump so you can work towards your purpose.

Diet and Exercise

Diet and exercise often fall by the wayside after a breakup because you are just too emotionally overwhelmed to take care of yourself. You don't have the energy to cook, so you order takeaway or snack on junk food. You need a quick mood boost, so you look for sugary foods and caffeine and you neglect your daily servings of vegetables. You don't have any drive for working out, so you decide to spend the evening curled up on the couch instead, or you sleep in instead of going to the gym on the weekends. As a result, your physical well-being suffers, which makes it even more difficult to manage your emotional needs. When you don't feel well physically, it's only natural that you won't feel well mentally either. If you resort to comfort food and put off your workout routine in the hopes that you're taking a break and going easy on yourself, you're actually sabotaging your ability to feel better.

The FCP method can help you bounce back and manage your nutritional needs, as well as encourage a healthy level of exercise. Methods that encourage focus, such as creating routines and changing your environment, can also assist with maintaining physical fitness. When you create and stick to a routine, you can budget time for cooking a healthy meal and exercising, and you'll hold yourself to these promises. Making changes to your environment can include getting rid of tempting snacks and encouraging healthy eating by keeping the fridge and pantry well-stocked. You can even try moving exercise equipment so it's within your line of sight, which serves as a subtle reminder to stick to your workout routine.

Control and purpose play important roles here too. You'll need a good foundation of self-control to stick to these healthy routines and avoid snacking and slacking. This will help you resist engaging in unhealthy diet and exercise habits when you're having a bad day. Don't forget to motivate yourself to take care of your body by thinking about your personal goals as well. When you work to achieve physical fitness, it's not just about keeping off extra pounds or looking better. It's about feeling better and keeping yourself in top condition, so you have the energy and good health you need to live a long and happy life. Recognising the long-term benefits of prioritising your health can make it easier to stick to good habits, even when you're not feeling your best.

Spirituality

If you're a spiritual person, you may find yourself questioning your faith in the wake of a breakup. It is normal to get angry at higher powers when you're grieving, as you wonder why something so terrible would be allowed to happen. This is even more likely if you were in a toxic or abusive relationship, which can cause serious psychological trauma. You may feel abandoned by your faith, angry, frustrated, and upset, which can lead you to start seeing the world as a colder, crueller place and interfere with your sense of spirituality.

During these moments of doubt, you may find it helpful to rely on your community for support and understanding. Finding your sense of purpose can help you reconnect with others within your faith, while learning focus and control can make it easier to come to terms with what happened and forgive those who hurt you when you're ready. You may also discover a newfound sense of purpose through questioning and then reaffirming your personal beliefs. Oftentimes people finally start the healing process when they're working to help others, so engaging in charity events and having spiritual discussions can help you rediscover your place in the world.

Hobbies

The FCP method is excellent at helping you create and keep up with hobbies. When you experience any significant life event, hobbies can fall by the wayside. They're not absolutely vital to your survival, and if you're not in a good place mentally, the idea of working on anything you don't have to can sound less than appealing. However, hobbies are a great way to start feeling passionate and motivated again when you're down.

When you try a hobby, you open yourself up to the possibility of failure by attempting something new or working to increase your skills. It's okay to fail, though, because there are very few stakes since you only do hobbies for your own benefit. No one will yell at you if you mess up, and you have a safe place to gradually improve your competency and, as a result, your feelings of control. From here, you may turn your hobby into something that helps you give your life purpose, primarily through sharing it with others when you feel comfortable. The simple act of being able to point to something and say "I made that" can be a huge confidence booster when your life is in such an uncertain place. Even if you decide to keep your hobby to yourself for the time being, a creative pursuit like making art or journaling can be a great tool for sharpening your focus, as these hobbies encourage self-reflection and the ability to live in the moment as you express your thoughts and feelings.

Career Success

Finding success in most career paths essentially requires high levels of focus, control, and purpose. This is especially true after a breakup, where it can be very difficult to focus on your work when you're struggling to manage your emotions. Every time you sit down to work on a project, your thoughts may drift, and any negative self-talk can undermine your confidence in your ability to continue producing high-quality work. Additionally, if you don't have a good idea of what you want to accomplish with your life, you may find it difficult to stay engaged at work. Your job can serve as a stepping stone for bigger and better career moves that help you enrich the lives of your family and your community, but it's tough to recognise this if you lack purpose; instead, you may see it as a tedious affair, which leads to resentment, dissatisfaction, and low-quality work.

As you learn to cultivate focus, control, and purpose, there's a good chance you'll feel more capable and driven in regards to your work. Focus will allow you to tackle your to-do list one task at a time, completing everything to the best of your abilities and showcasing your skills to your boss. Control helps remind you that you are more than capable of succeeding and excelling at your job, and it can encourage you to take advantage of big opportunities for career growth. Purpose keeps you going, helping you recover from minor setbacks and encouraging you to focus on the big picture rather than getting bogged down in the day-to-day annoyances. With the FCP method, not only will you prevent a breakup from interfering with your ability to work, but you'll also have all the motivation you need to find even greater career success than before.

Family Life

It can occasionally be hard to stay in touch with your family after a breakup. You may not feel up to socialising in general, even though you know that talking through the problems you're facing with supportive people would likely help you process them. You may also have trouble finding the energy to take care of kids if you have them, or to spend time with them when you would really rather curl up in bed and block out the world for a few hours. While wanting some alone time every once in a while is natural, your responsibilities as a parent do not cease to exist when you're not feeling well, and reaching out to friends and family when you're down can often be the best move for maintaining a positive mindset.

When in doubt, remind yourself that part of your purpose is loving your family and working to provide them with a better life. You cannot do that if you let yourself get buried under stress, shame, and doubt. Make an effort to engage with their lives, allowing them to support you and supporting them in turn when you have regained the focus and control necessary to do so.

Chapter 9: Real-World Examples of People who Recovered From Toxic Relationships

When you experience a toxic relationship and difficult breakup, you may feel like no one understands what you're going through. Your pain is so deep that you might become convinced that you'll never recover, and you'll have to struggle to deal with the trauma caused by the relationship for the rest of your life. It can seem like there's no way out and no way for the situation to get better. However, time heals all wounds, and you can and will get back on your feet once you've given yourself the time and opportunity to heal. After all, many people have come out of toxic relationships and gone on to have very successful lives.

Among celebrities, there are many who have experienced pain and heartbreak in their lives. While they likely shared the same doubts and fears you did, they ended up coming out the other side of the experience stronger than ever, ready to make their mark on their world. They used the breakup as a chance to grow as people, and it often helped them discover their passion and purpose. Notable celebrities who were once in toxic relationships include Mariah Carey, Reese Witherspoon, and Jennifer Lopez.

Mariah Carey

Mariah Carey may be best known for her music and rise to stardom, but this doesn't mean she's never experienced any difficulty in her life. In her 2020 memoir *The Meaning of Mariah Carey*, she shares many of the harrowing experiences she's faced, including her experience with an abusive relationship. Carey married 43-year-old music producer Tommy Mottola when she was only 23, and this helped to solidify a significant power imbalance between the two of them.

Despite Carey's fame, Mottola attempted to control various aspects of her life, including attempting to cut her off from her friends and the rest of her support network. She claims that she wasn't allowed to speak to people without Mottola's approval, and that she didn't feel safe or comfortable in her own home. The situation became so bad that Carey recounts how she kept a "to-go" bag stocked and her purse filled with essentials just in case she ever needed to leave in a hurry. The fear she felt from her ex's attempts to control her made it impossible for Carey to live in a way that was true to herself, but luckily, Carey was able to end the relationship, going on to continue singing and entertaining her fans. Of this time in her life, Carey said, "Captivity and control come in many forms, but the goal is always the same—to break down the captive's will, to kill any notion of self-worth and erase the person's memory of their own soul [...] But thankfully, I smuggled myself out bit by bit, through the lyrics of my songs" (Carey & Davis, 2020). She was able to turn her purpose into her reason for living, recovering from her experience in an abusive relationship through her music.

Carey's situation was especially difficult for her to navigate because she and Mottola shared a business relationship on top of a personal one. This encouraged her to remain in the relationship for four years, even though she knew it was causing her harm to do so. This is a similar story to many people who aren't able to support themselves financially, or who might share their business or social circles with their spouse and may be afraid to end the relationship as a result. This added to the control Carey claims Mottola had over her life, but despite this and the many other hardships Carey has faced, the end of her relationship did not spell the end for her. She learned to work through her emotions and manage the trauma that such a difficult period of her life had caused, all while living in the limelight. She continues to write and record music, go on tours, and live the life of a celebrity, unwilling to allow her past to define her. Carey doesn't deny the seriousness of what she experienced, but she doesn't let it hold her back from living her life the way she wants to, just as you shouldn't let your past relationship hold you back either.

Reese Witherspoon

Reese Witherspoon has repeatedly made headlines throughout her career as an actress and producer, but in 2018, she made headlines for a different reason entirely. During an interview with Oprah Winfrey, Witherspoon described her experience in a relationship in her youth that she characterised as verbally and psychologically abusive. While Witherspoon doesn't give specific information about who her abusive ex is or what exactly she experienced during the relationship, she notes that part of the reason for her leaving the relationship was that she attempted to set boundaries, and when those boundaries were repeatedly and severely crossed, she knew she had to get out for her own safety. She was losing control, which made it difficult for her to find the courage to leave. Later in the interview, Witherspoon noted how "it changed who I was on a cellular level, the fact that I stood up for myself," as well as how "leaving those situations isn't easy because it's wrought with self-doubt, particularly if someone damages your self-esteem [...] I didn't have self-esteem, you know? And I'm a different person now" (OWN,

2018). The toxicity of the relationship undermined Witherspoon's ability to feel in control of her own life and to stand up for herself. At the same time, it was only by pushing through this barrier and finding the courage to leave that she was able to get her life back on track.

Witherspoon's story speaks to the fact that no matter who you are, it is incredibly tough to leave an abusive relationship, and yet it is also incredibly rewarding. She recounts the story as a response to Oprah's question, "What's the most difficult decision you had to make to fulfill your destiny?" (OWN, 2018). This alludes to Witherspoon's perspective on her breakup. It was incredibly difficult, and she likely felt all of the negative and confusing emotions you are currently experiencing. It's normal to be hesitant to leave even the worst of relationships because of that fear of being on your own, and the dependency you begin to feel towards your controlling partner. Still, Witherspoon sees leaving the relationship as, ultimately, a positive force in her life. She notes that it was something she had to do to achieve her destiny, showcasing how finding her purpose was part of her recovery process, just like in the FCP method. Witherspoon could have spent all her time looking back, undermining her future endeavours with the self-doubt she acquired from her rocky relationship. Instead, she chose to focus on improving herself in the present moment, unlearning the harmful ideas and behaviours she picked up over the years and forging her path to success.

Jennifer Lopez

Jennifer Lopez has had an extensive career as a celebrity, rising to stardom as a dancer and later pursuing both singing and acting. She has also experienced multiple difficult and often toxic relationships where her partner attempted to undermine her feelings of self-worth and manipulate her emotions. Lopez characterises these relationships as "mentally, emotionally, and verbally" (Taylor, 2014) abusive, specifically in regards to her relationship with singer-songwriter Marc Anthony. She notes that while the relationship never escalated to physical abuse, it was still toxic and very damaging, showcasing how other kinds of abuse that tend to slip under the radar can be just as serious.

Despite the difficulties she faced, Lopez has not allowed the end of her seven-year marriage to hold her back from pursuing what she loves. In fact, she has repeatedly engaged with the topic of abuse in her work, finding a sense of purpose in covering these stories for a wider audience and being honest about her past experiences. Just one year after her divorce, Lopez went on her Dance Again tour, which aimed to shed light on abusive relationships, the damage they do, and how people who have been victims of abuse can still go on to lead fulfilling and rewarding lives. By allowing her experiences to influence her art, Lopez began to regain the focus and control over her life that she felt she had lost during her relationship, funnelling these into the sense of purpose she's found in entertaining and educating others.

Perhaps Lopez's most notable way of channelling her past into her purpose is through her memoir, *True Love*, where she recounts the two-year period in her life during which she "confronted her greatest challenges, identified her biggest fears, and ultimately emerged a stronger person than she's ever been" (Lopez, 2015). By providing this behind-the-scenes look at her life and the difficulties she experienced in her past familial and romantic relationships, Lopez is able to open up about her past and educate others who may be in the same position she was. She focuses on the work she had to do to grow and heal after leaving her relationship, and how she found inspiration from her own work. Her journey of self-discovery and change was highly influential to the type of person she has become since the end of her relationship and the career goals she has pursued.

Each of the women discussed in this chapter have experienced hardships from their toxic relationships. They have had moments of self-doubt and uncertainty that kept them tethered to these relationships, but they also found the courage to leave them. None of them allowed these moments to end their careers. Instead, they pursued self-discovery and growth. They saw the end of their relationships not as something to mourn or something that held them back forever, but as a reason to keep moving forward. This is what you must do as well. You will have moments of fear, worry, and hesitancy. There will be points in your life when you wonder if you will suffer from the negative effects of your past relationships forever. It is tempting to give in to these fears, but if the stories covered in this chapter tell you anything, it should be that a toxic relationship or even a bad breakup doesn't mean you can never lead a successful and fulfilling life. On the contrary, the growth and recovery you engage in after the relationship can be just what you need to discover your life's purpose and start working towards it.

Conclusion

As the famous saying goes, "when one door closes, another one opens." A breakup represents the end of one era of your life, and it's difficult to leave it behind. It's natural to feel shaken, hurt, angry, resentful, or betrayed. Toxic and otherwise unbalanced relationships can make it even more difficult to cope with the period of uncertainty that follows a breakup. You may feel lost and confused, unsure of where to go from here. You may wish to turn back time, but the unfortunate reality of the situation is that this just isn't possible. Still, this doesn't mean your life is over. Yes, the relationship has ended, but there is still plenty for you to experience and accomplish. You have your whole life ahead of you, and your future can be far brighter than your past if you work to make it so.

Throughout this book, you've learned how to better parse your feelings after a breakup, coming to terms with confusing and conflicting feelings like a loss of security, low self-esteem, and difficulty rediscovering your identity as an individual. You've looked at a breakup through the lens of grief, understanding how each of the five stages can come into play and how to manage them as they appear. You've learned that you're not alone, and that there are plenty of positive role models in the celebrity world and likely in your own social circles who have experienced the pain of a breakup and managed to heal over time. Perhaps most importantly, you were introduced to the FCP tripod method, which provides you with the tools you need to really come to terms with your breakup and start to move on from it.

As you begin the next chapter of your life, remember how the values of focus, control, and purpose can make all the difference. These qualities are catalysts for positive change, and they can help turn the confusion and distress that comes from the end of a relationship into personal growth and a more fulfilling life. You practise focus every time you quell ruminating thoughts and bring your mind back to the present so you can be more productive and present in your life. You practise control every time you counter self-doubt with affirmations of your worth, turning uncertainty into confidence and a drive to succeed. You practise purpose every time you let go of your uncertainty and regrets so you can set goals and work towards achieving them, giving yourself a newfound sense of motivation when you need it most. With the FCP method, you can pick up the pieces after a breakup and not only fix the damage the breakup caused, but come out of the experience better than ever before, ready to take on life with confidence and a smile.

You are much stronger than you know. Don't let your doubts get the best of you, and remember that you have worth as an individual, not just as one part of a matching set.

You may go on to enter into a relationship again, but it should be on your own terms, and with a partner who you truly love. Remind yourself of your value while working each day to improve yourself, and you will find that you can create a fulfilling life for yourself, whether you're in a loving and equal relationship or even on your own. It is possible to find success after a breakup, no matter how low you may be feeling right now. Use your breakup as a springboard to personal growth and fulfilment. Navigate the world with focus, control, and purpose. Rediscover yourself, and you will find that in a few weeks or months, you will truly be over your breakup and onto bigger and better things.

References

11417994. (2019, Jan. 28). *Woman in the mountains*. Pixabay. https://pixabay.com/photos/mountains-canada-girl-outlook-snow-3959204/

Avi_acl. (2017, Apr. 19). *Woman facing the sunrise*. Pixabay. https://pixabay.com/photos/morning-sunrise-woman-silhouette-2243465/

Bob_Dmyt. (2019, Oct. 6). *Teamwork hands-in*. Pixabay. https://pixabay.com/photos/team-friendship-group-hands-4529717/

Brenner, A. (2019, July 30). *9 ways to help you process the loss of a love relationship*. Psychology Today. https://www.psychologytoday.com/us/blog/in-flux/201907/9-ways-help-you-process-the-loss-love-relationship

Carey, M. & Davis, M. A. (2020, Sept. 29). *The meaning of Mariah Carey*. Andy Cohen Books.

Cleveland Clinic. (2019, Jan. 23). *Grieving after a break-up? 6 strategies to help you heal*. HealthEssentials. https://health.clevelandclinic.org/grieving-after-a-break-up-6-strategies-to-help-you-heal/

Dodgson, L. (2019, Oct. 27). *A 'get your ex back' website conducted research to find out what really happens to couples who rekindle their romance*. Insider. https://www.insider.com/what-happens-when-couples-get-back-together-after-a-breakup-2019-10

Free-Photos. (2016, Jan. 7). *Woman sitting at the window*. Pixabay. https://pixabay.com/photos/window-view-sitting-girl-indoors-1081788/

Geller, S. (2013, Dec. 5). *The psychology of self-motivation | Scott Geller | TEDxVirginiaTech* [Video]. YouTube. https://www.youtube.com/watch?v=7sxpKhIbroE

Graham, S. (2002, Jan. 15). *Study shows that, for women, suppressing emotions increases anger*. Scientific American. https://www.scientificamerican.com/article/study-shows-that-for-wome/

Jonas-svidras. (2017, Dec. 29). *Camera lens focus*. Pixabay. https://pixabay.com/photos/lens-camera-taking-photos-3046269/

Kübler-Ross, E. (1969). *On death and dying*: *What the dying have to teach doctors, nurses, clergy, & their own families*. The Macmillan Company.

Leipzig, A. (2013, Feb. 1). *How to know your life purpose in 5 minutes | Adam Leipzig | TEDxMalibu* [Video]. YouTube. https://www.youtube.com/watch?v=vVsXO9brK7M

LoboStudioHamburg. (2014, March 23). *Social media apps*. Pixabay. https://pixabay.com/photos/phone-display-apps-applications-292994/

Lopez, J. (2015, Nov. 3). *True love*. Celebra.

Mwitt1337. (2017, May 4). *Business meeting*. Pixabay. https://pixabay.com/photos/meeting-business-architect-office-2284501/

OWN. (2018, Feb. 6). *Reese Witherspoon on the abusive relationship that changed her | SuperSoul Sunday | OWN* [Video]. YouTube. https://www.youtube.com/watch?v=3CR7EeK-zUA

Pavlofox. (2016, Aug. 3). *Curled fist*. Pixabay. https://pixabay.com/photos/fist-blow-power-wrestling-violence-1561157/

Pexels. (2016, Nov. 29). *Family at the beach*. Pixabay. https://pixabay.com/photos/beach-family-fun-leisure-ocean-1867271/

Pexels. (2016, Nov. 22). *Woman meditating*. Pixabay. https://pixabay.com/photos/meditate-woman-yoga-zen-meditating-1851165/

PhotoMIX-Company. (2018, Feb. 12). *Heart hands*. Pixabay. https://pixabay.com/photos/heart-love-sunset-shape-sign-3147976/

Picjumbo_com. (2015, July 30). *Woman writing in a journal*. Pixabay. https://pixabay.com/photos/female-diary-journal-write-865110/

RyanMcGuire. (2014, Aug. 8). *Girl sitting on bench*. Pixabay. https://pixabay.com/photos/worried-girl-woman-waiting-sitting-413690/

Sasint. (2016, Nov. 11). *Climbing together*. Pixabay. https://pixabay.com/photos/sunset-men-silhouettes-helping-1807524/

Silviarita. (2017, Sept. 16). *Making a salad*. Pixabay. https://pixabay.com/photos/salad-fruits-berries-healthy-2756467/

Smith, I. (2018, Dec. 14). *Goal review*. Unsplash. https://unsplash.com/photos/8XlMU62ii8I

Stevepb. (2015, Jan. 28). *Scheduling*. Pixabay. https://pixabay.com/photos/diary-journal-pen-notebook-january-614149/

StockSnap. (2017, Aug. 5). *Making a checklist*. Pixabay. https://pixabay.com/photos/checklist-goals-box-notebook-pen-2589418/

Taylor, D. B. (2014, Oct. 29). *J.Lo: I've been mentally, emotionally and verbally abused*. Page Six. https://pagesix.com/2014/10/29/j-lo-ive-been-mentally-emotionally-and-verbally-abused/

Victorvote. (2019, Dec. 4). *Man crying*. Pixabay. https://pixabay.com/photos/crying-crying-man-sadness-cry-sad-4670799/

Walesh, S. G. (n.d.). *Using the power of habits to work smarter*. Helping You Engineer Your Future. http://www.helpingyouengineeryourfuture.com/habits-work-smarter.htm

Printed in Great Britain
by Amazon

79097027R00058